Salsas!

By Andrea Chesman

The Crossing Press / Freedom, California 95019

Library of Congress Cataloging-in-Publication Data

Chesman, Andrea.
  Salsas!

  Includes index.
  1. Salsas (Cookery) I. Title
TX819.S29C47 1985 641.6′384 85-17114
ISBN 0-89594-179-1
ISBN 0-89594-178-3 (pbk.)

Acknowledgments

I'd like to thank Elaine Gill for presenting me with the idea for this cookbook, as well as for her support and encouragement. Special thanks go to Richard Ruane for his enthusiastic tasting of all the recipes that went into this cookbook, as well as the recipes that did not go in, and for his support and practical help throughout the writing of this book.

Preface

In Spanish, the word "salsa" means sauce. To many of us, whose first introduction to fiery Tex-Mex cooking included a dip into a hot chile-pepper-and-tomato-based table sauce, salsa has come to mean hot sauce.

Eating with hot sauces is a warming experience—the sensation starts at the tip of the lips, and travels all through the head (occasionally lifting off the top of the head), finally leaving a warm glow in the belly.

Chile peppers, the basis for these wonderful sauces, originated in South America and were brought to Europe by Spanish explorers. From Europe, chiles spread rapidly to Africa and the Far East where they were readily adapted and incorporated into the native cuisines.

The recipes in this cookbook are for people who love the taste of hot foods. Ranging from quite hot to mildly hot, the recipes represent a hot sauce express through a few different cuisines. However, I make no claim for each recipe's authenticity. While many of the hot sauces are classics, many more are products of inspiration and locally available ingredients. Although some of the recipes may call for hard to find ingredients (all of which are available through the mail, see page 128 for sources), most have been designed to be made quickly and easily from readily available ingredients.

I have tried to be as flexible as possible about which chile peppers to use in a specific recipe. I live in Vermont, which is not exactly a center of chile agriculture. In the summer, I can grow a few varieties (with a little bit of luck and sunshine) or I can find some unusual varieties at the farmer's market. During the winter, the supermarket stocks a ubiquitous "hot pepper," which is sometimes a cayenne pepper, sometimes a California green chile.

Jalapeños are often available, too. So, many recipes often call for "hot peppers," when a fresh chile is required. By using different varieties of chiles, the flavor of the recipe may vary each time, but the recipes will work and be pleasing, regardless of the chile variety you use.

Likewise, when it comes to hotness, you are in charge. There's no point in seasoning foods with so much chile pepper that you don't enjoy it. Hot foods should be stimulating to the palate, not overwhelming. If your palate is sensitive to hot foods (it is an acquired taste), go easy on the chiles. It is perfectly acceptable to substitute a mild-flavored chile (including a sweet bell pepper) for a hot one. The flavor of the recipe will vary considerably from the original, but the results will still be flavorful. Pass a bottle of concentrated hot sauce at the table for those who want their foods hotter.

Most of the recipes in this cookbook take very little time to prepare. One chapter contains recipes for various different salsas. Most of these salsas are meant to be served at the table as a relish or condiment. Some of these sauces can be made up in quantities, then frozen or canned for long-term storage. The remaining chapters contain recipes which utilize salsas as a sauce or seasoning base. With plenty of salsas stocked in the refrigerator, you may find yourself using them in every possible dish—as I do. This cookbook can get you started on ways to incorporate hot sauces into your favorite dishes—classic and original.

Contents

1.

ABOUT CHILES

This is really a book about chiles—the basic ingredient of all salsas.

Chiles, or peppers, are members of the *Capsicum* family. They originated in South America, possibly Brazil, and are not at all related to the pepper (*Piper nigrum*) of the salt-and-pepper variety. The Aztecs called them "chilli."

Chiles were used by the Aztecs at least as far back as 700 B.C. They were prepared in cooked dishes and used medicinally to treat colds, malaria, indigestion, toothaches, and colic. It was said that chiles could clarify the blood and promote robust health. It was also used as a stimulant for the romantically disinclined. Modern scientists will agree that chiles, eaten in moderation, have a beneficial affect on digestion. Ground cayenne pepper is sometimes packed into capsules and prescribed for upset stomachs. Chiles are low in calories and contain vitamins A, B, C, and E.

It was Columbus who caused the name confusion (chile vs. pepper) by reporting back to Queen Isabella that he had tasted a "pepper more pungent than that of the Caucasus." Always eager for spices, the Europeans readily adopted chiles, as the Spanish came to call them.

From the Mediterranean where chiles were most popular, the new spice was readily spread to Africa, Indonesian, and China, where chiles are the cornerstone of Szechuan cooking, and India, where they became so popular and so commonly grown, some botanists thought chiles were indigenous.

Botanists are still a little confused about chiles. Some say there are only two species of chiles (*C. annum*, which includes the sweet varieties, and *C. frutescens*, which includes most of the hot varieties). Other botanists recognize about 25 different species. Regardless of the botanical controversies, cooks easily can recognize that there is a great variety of chiles to cook with, and the choice of a chile in a dish can affect its flavor, as well as its hotness.

Chile Varieties

A number of different chiles are used in cooking Mexican foods and in preparing different salsas. It is not always easy to keep chiles straight.

For one thing, it isn't that easy to taste the differences among chiles, particularly in their dried state. But even fresh chiles can taste confusingly similar, because the hot flavor can overwhelm the palate. Also chiles of the same variety can have different degrees of hotness. Growing conditions, climate, and altitude will all affect flavor. For another, it isn't always easy to recognize a chile from a written description. Size and color can be counted on to vary from the description. There is a final source of confusion: chile names can vary from region to region.

Given these limitations, here is a listing of some of the more common chiles to help you make some selections.

Dried Chiles

Ancho (Sometimes called pasilla, sometimes called pisado). These are ripened and dried chile poblanos. They are recognized by their large rounded shape, dark mahogany color, and wrinkled skin. Fairly mild but full-flavored, ancho chiles are frequently ground to make chili powder.

Arbol. These "tree chiles" are fairly small (2½ inches long or so), narrow, and very hot.

California Dried Chiles. These smooth-skinned chiles are dried Anaheim chiles. They are rather mild in flavor.

Cascabels. So named because they sound like rattles when they are shaken, cascabels are small, round, hot chiles.

Chipotles. These chiles are ripened, smoke-dried jalapeños. Sometimes they can be found canned. They are very hot and add a wonderful smoky flavor to dishes. There are no substitutes for these chiles.

Guajillos. Long, slender chiles with pointed tips. Their brown-red skin is shiny and tough.

Japónes. Very hot in flavor, these are dried serrano chiles.

New Mexico Red Chiles. Chiles from New Mexico are said to be hotter than California chiles. These are similar in appearance to California red chiles. Both are often sold on strings (chile de ristra).

Pasillas. Small slender chiles with rounded tips, these chiles have hot seeds but fairly mild flesh.

Pequíns. Also called tepíns, these tiny bright red chiles are *very* hot.

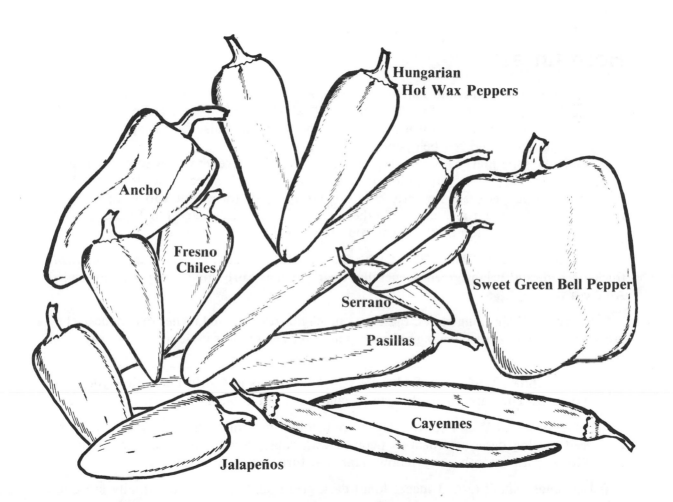

Hungarian
Hot Wax Peppers

Ancho

Fresno
Chiles

Serrano

Pasillas

Sweet Green Bell Pepper

Cayennes

Jalapeños

Fresh Chiles

You probably won't find much variety among the fresh hot peppers you find in the supermarket. In Vermont, I find "hot peppers," which are California green chiles, quite mild in flavor, or cayennes, which can be either hot or mild. I also find jalapeños, and of course, sweet green and red bell peppers.

While the supermarkets are limited, home gardeners are likely to grow some interesting varieties of hot peppers—even in the northern climes. Johnny's Selected Seeds has specially developed hot pepper seeds for early-maturing crops. Seeds for a wide variety of hot peppers are available from a number of other seed companies (see page 130 for addresses). Here's a brief description of the chiles you are most likely to encounter.

California Green Chiles. These peppers are widely available. They are long, firm, thick-fleshed, and bright green. Generally, their flavor is fairly mild. They are also called Anaheims.

Cayennes. Thin, long chiles, these vary in length from about 4 inches to 8 inches. They are a light green in color, turning red as they mature. The hotness varies tremendously from pepper to pepper.

Fresno Chiles. You'll only find these *very hot* peppers in California, unless you grow them yourself. They are about the size of jalapeños, but conical in shape.

Hungarian Hot Wax Peppers. These are medium hot chiles, popular with gardeners. One seed catalog describes them as peppers with "authority." The chiles are about 5½ inches long, with smooth waxy yellow skins that turn red upon maturity.

Jalapeños. Small (2½–3 inches long) dark green chiles, jalapeños usually are quite

6

hot. Generally, the smaller the jalapeño, the hotter the flavor. They are often available canned. It has been my experience that the canned jalapeños vary in hotness as much as the fresh jalapeños. Also, they pack tighter in a measuring cup. When a recipe calls for a certain measure of jalapeños, use less if you are using canned ones.

Serrano. Very small, very hot, light green chiles. These are also available canned.

Sweet Green Bell Peppers. These sweet, box-shaped chiles are almost always available. You can cut the hotness of any recipe by substituting green bell pepper.

Sweet Red Bell Peppers. When a green bell pepper is fully mature, it becomes a red bell pepper. They are often quite expensive. Substitute canned red bell peppers, pimientos, or green bell peppers.

A Warning About Handling Chiles

Chiles contain an oil, capsaicin, that can be very irritating to the skin. Most of this irritating substance is contained in the veins or ribs that run near the seeds. When you handle large quantities of chiles, wear gloves to protect your hands, and never, never touch your hands (or gloves) to your face. The oils can cause painful burns. If you should accidentally come in contact with the irritating substance, wash the affected part thoroughly with soapy water.

The effect of the capsaicin is cumulative. You may not notice the burn until it is too late. I once thought I was immune to the burn. Foolishly, I seeded a lot of chiles by running my thumb down their insides. About an hour later, I had a fierce burning sensation under my thumbnail that no amount of washing relieved (How do you wash under a thumbnail?).

The throbbing pain lasted for more than a day. I seed fresh chiles with the rounded tip of a vegetable peeler. It works very well.

Roasting Fresh Chiles

Roasting fresh chiles enhances the flavor and enables you to slip off the skins.

If you are roasting only 1 chile, it is easiest to slip the chile onto a long-handled fork or barbecue skewer and hold the chile over a hot burner of a gas or electric stove. Hold the chile a few inches over the burner and turn the chile as it chars and blisters.

If you are roasting more than 1 chile, place the chiles on a baking sheet under a pre-heated broiler about 4–6 inches from the flame. Broil, turning frequently, until the chiles are blistered and slightly charred.

Then place the chiles in a paper bag. Close the top of the bag and allow the peppers to steam for about 10 minutes. This loosens the skins. Remove from the bag and slide the skins off. You may need to use a sharp knife on some varieties to peel the skins. Pull off the stems. By pulling the stems away from the chile, rather than twisting them off, you should be able to remove most of the seeds and veins along with the stem. Slit open the chiles and scrape away the remaining seeds and veins, if desired.

Storing and Handling Dried Chiles

While a string of dried chiles makes a wonderful kitchen decoration, the heat, dust, and humidity in most kitchens do not do much to maintain the quality of the chiles. You can store dried chiles in any cool dry place. I find I get best results by storing the chiles in carefully sealed plastic bags in the freezer.

Before cooking any dried chile, wipe it off with a clean moist cloth to remove any surface dust. If you are presoaking a chile and planning to use the soaking water, use all but the last ¼ cup or so of the soaking water. Any dirt that remained on the chile will settle to the bottom of the soaking water.

If the skins of the chile are bitter, you can remove them by scraping the pulp from the skin. Discard both the skins and the soaking water in that case. Or press the final sauce through a nonaluminum metal sieve to remove pieces of skin.

Cooking in Nonaluminum Pots

Aluminum reacts with acids. It will *definitely* react with the acids in peppers. Don't even bother to make salsas that require more than a few minutes of cooking if you have aluminum cookware. The salsas will develop a strong metallic taste. The same taste will develop if you strain a salsa through an aluminum strainer. Use enamel-coated or stainless steel cookware where chiles are concerned.

Buying Fresh Chiles

When buying fresh chiles, look for signs of freshness. The chiles should be firm to the touch. The skins should not be wrinkled or wilted. There should be no bruises, bad spots, or soft spots. Try to pick out ones with the most regular shape; they will be easier to handle in the kitchen. Generally, the smaller the chile, the hotter, so select accordingly.

When you get the chiles home, store them in the refrigerator in a paper bag or wrapped in paper towels, or both. They should keep for a week or more. Chiles stored in plastic bags will become slimy to the touch and are very prone to rapid spoilage.

Long-term Storage of Fresh Chiles

If you see a bargain of fresh chiles, or if you harvest your own surplus, you may want to preserve some by freezing or pickling, rather than drying.

Freezing Fresh Chiles

My favorite method of preserving fresh chiles is by freezing. I make the process as simple as possible. First I wash the chiles and dry them thoroughly. They must be completely dry before they are frozen. Then I split the chiles in half, seed them, chop them, and lay them in a single layer on a baking sheet. The tray goes into the freezer to quickly freeze the chiles. Once they are frozen, I bag them. The chiles remain loose and can be removed from the bag in any quantity when you are ready to use them. This method takes very little time, and the frozen chiles can be added directly to a sauce. The drawback is that the skins become a little tough so they are not very good in uncooked salsas.

For a slightly improved product, you can roast the chiles first (see page 8 for instructions). Then tray freeze the whole chiles. The skins will slip off when the chiles are defrosted. Deforst and peel the chiles before adding them to a sauce.

Pickling Fresh Chiles

Pickling is an excellent way to preserve chiles. You can't use pickled chiles in every salsa, but some are enhanced by the presence of pickled chiles (see Pickled Pepper Salsa, page 18). Pickled peppers make excellent garnishes; they can be sprinkled on sandwiches, nachos, pizzas, or wherever your desire leads you. You can substitute pickled chiles for un-pickled chiles in salsas. Of course, the flavor will be radically different, but the recipe will still work as long as you omit any lemon juice or vinegar that the recipe requires.

Pickled Peppers I

First prepare your canning jars and lids according to the manufacturer's instructions. For each quart of chiles, heat 1½ cups white vinegar and 1 cup water. While the brine heats, place 1 teaspoon salt and 1 teaspoon sugar (optional) in each clean hot quart canning jar. You can also add a clove of garlic if you like. Pack with the peppers, leaving ½ inch head space at the top. Pour in the hot brine to cover the peppers, leaving ¼ inch head space. Seal with a 2-piece metal canning lid. Process in a boiling water bath for 10 minutes. Cool undisturbed for 12 hours. Store in a cool, dry place. Plan to use the peppers within a year.

The same oil in peppers, capsaicin, which can be very irritating to the hands, seems to eat the rubber seal on canned chiles on occasion. So check your jars often for broken seals. As with all canned goods, do not eat the contents of a jar with a broken seal. Throw the chiles out where humans and animals won't be tempted to try them.

Opened jars should be stored in the refrigerator. The seal may deteriorate in the refrigerator. In that case, simply replace the lid. You will know if the peppers have gone bad. They will have an off odor, be slimy to the touch, be fuzzy, or have a white sediment in the brine and covering the peppers. If any of these symptoms characterize your peppers, throw them out. More likely than not, you won't have any trouble with spoilage.

Pickled Peppers II

Even if you don't have a canner, you can still make pickled peppers. These peppers will keep for several months in a cool dark place, such as a cellar.

To make 1 quart of pickled peppers, cut a slit in each chile. (This will prevent the pickle from squirting juice in your face when you bite into it and allow the vinegar to pickle the insides.) Pack the chiles, 1 teaspoon of salt, and a garlic clove if desired, into a hot sterilized canning jar. Heat 2½ cups of white vinegar to just below the boiling point. Pour the vinegar over the chiles. Fill the jar to within ¼ inch of the top with olive oil. Be sure the chiles are completely covered by the brine. You will need about ¼ cup of olive oil. Cap the jar with a 2-piece metal canning lid, but do not tighten the screw band. Store at a constant temperature of 60–70° F. for about 10 days. The chiles should be well pickled by then. Store in a cool, dry place.

2.
SALSA RECIPES

This chapter contains recipes for making 20 different salsas—some with fresh chiles, some with dried. Some are salsa crudas—uncooked salsas—some require slow simmering. Some contain tomatoes, some tomatillos, some just chiles. Something for everyone, I hope.

There is nothing difficult about making salsas. The salsa will be as good as the ingredients you start out with. A good salsa cruda always starts with vine-ripened tomatoes, home-grown or locally grown, if possible. Tomatoes that are picked green and ripened artificially (like most of the tomatoes that one finds in the supermarket in the winter) just won't make a decent tasting salsa. If you can't find vine-ripened tomatoes, substitute canned tomatoes, which are rich in flavor, if low in texture. A 1-pound can of tomatoes is roughly equivalent to 2 cups of fresh chopped tomatoes.

Some recipes call for peeled and seeded tomatoes. To peel a tomato, dip it in boiling water for about 30 seconds to loosen the skin. Then cool the tomato and peel away the skin with a sharp paring knife. To seed a tomato, slice the tomato in half and gently squeeze out the seeds.

I will confess that I do not always bother to peel and seed my tomatoes. The skins of tomatoes sometimes are tough in a salsa cruda. In a cooked salsa, they sometimes separate from the tomatoes. Then you get wisps of skin floating in the sauce. This is not as bad as it sounds; most people will never notice it. Same thing with the seeds. Some people just don't mind finding seeds in their salsa. So if you are feeling lazy or pressed for time, don't bother to peel and seed your tomatoes; you may not even notice the difference.

Feel free to substitute different chiles in the recipes. Those that are listed with each recipe have been tested—I know that those particular chiles will contribute a pleasing flavor to a salsa. I don't know how other chiles will taste, but I suspect they will work just fine. Substitute with the chile varieties you have on hand and see what happens.

I use a food processor for a lot of chopping and mixing. You can use a food processor fitted with a steel blade to chop vegetables for a salsa, but chop each ingredient separately.

Otherwise, the vegetables will be overprocessed and the texture will be too smooth. Also, the ingredients should be combined by hand. Mixing in the food processor incorporates too much air into the salsa and tends to overprocess the vegetables.

Because salsas are made from high-acid ingredients, they keep well in the refrigerator. Salsas should be stored in glass jars or glass or ceramic bowls, tightly covered. Most will keep for 1 week; many will keep for several weeks. Some of the salsas freeze well. Frozen salsas should be thawed completely and well mixed before using.

I prefer to can some salsas to have on hand at all times. The advantage of canning over freezing is that the salsa is ready to be used in the jar and doesn't require defrosting first. I have given instructions for canning with several recipes. If you have never canned before, you may want to consult another book for basic canning techniques. *Putting Food By* by Ruth Hertzberg, Beatrice Vaughan, and Janet Greene (Stephen Greene Press) is my favorite reference for food preservation techniques.

UNCOOKED SALSAS

Salsa Cruda

2 cups peeled, seeded,
  and chopped tomatoes
½ cup finely chopped scallions,
  including the green tops
¼ cup finely chopped
  fresh hot pepper
¼ cup finely chopped
  sweet green pepper
2 teaspoons finely chopped cilantro
  (optional)
⅛ teaspoon sugar (optional)
Salt and pepper

There's not much variation in recipes for Salsa Cruda. The real secret lies in using the very best, very ripest homegrown tomatoes. If you don't have vine-ripened fresh tomatoes, you may be better off using canned ones; the flavor of most supermarket tomatoes is too insipid to use in this salsa.

Chop each ingredient by hand. Or chop each ingredient separately in a food processor fitted with a steel blade; do not overprocess. Mix all the ingredients together. Taste and adjust the seasonings. Let the salsa stand for at least 30 minutes. Stir well before serving.

Yield: Approximately 2 cups

Busy Person Salsa

1 (1-pound) can peeled
   and seeded tomatoes, drained
¼ cup chopped onion
1 garlic clove, minced
1 (4-ounce) can chopped
   green chilies, drained
¼ teaspoon sugar
1 teaspoon vinegar
Salt
Really Hot Pepper Sauce (page 30)
   or Louisiana Red Hot Sauce(page 35)

Although I prefer to make my uncooked salsas with fresh tomatoes and to chop each ingredient by hand, when time is short, or when the vegetables aren't in season, I turn to canned tomatoes and chiles. This recipe can be made in about 2 minutes in a blender or food processor. It can be used in any recipe calling for Salsa Cruda; but it is best in cooked dishes. It makes a good enchilada sauce.

Combine all the ingredients in a blender or food processor. Process very briefly until the salsa is mixed but not too smooth. Taste and adjust seasonings. If possible, allow to sit for 30 minutes to allow the flavors to blend.

Yield: Approximately 2½ cups

17

Pickled Pepper Salsa

5 cups peeled, seeded,
  and finely chopped tomatoes
½ cup chopped pickled jalapeños,
  including some pickling liquid
1 onion, finely chopped
1 scallion, including some green top,
  finely chopped
2 teaspoons chopped fresh cilantro
Salt

Chop each ingredient by hand. Or chop each ingredient separately in a food processor fitted with a steel blade. Then combine all the ingredients, adding salt to taste. Allow to stand for about 1 hour to allow the flavors to blend. Stir well before serving.

Yield: Approximately 5 cups

Avocado Salsa Cruda

½ cup finely diced avocado
1½ cups peeled, seeded,
   and finely chopped tomatoes
   (about 2 tomatoes)
½ cup finely diced red onion
¼ cup finely diced jalapeño
¼ cup finely diced
   sweet green pepper
¼ cup chopped fresh parsley
⅛ teaspoon sugar (optional)
Salt

Chop each vegetable by hand or with a food processor fitted with a steel blade. Mix together in a nonaluminum bowl. Add the sugar and salt to taste. Adjust the seasonings if necessary. Let the salsa sit for at least 1 hour. Stir well before serving.

Yield: Approximately 2 cups

Tomatillo Salsa

1 small onion, finely chopped
2 garlic cloves, minced
¼ cup chopped pickled jalapeño
  peppers
2 tablespoons chopped fresh cilantro
  (optional)
1 (13-ounce) can tomatillos, drained
Pinch sugar (optional)

A moderately hot salsa. It's great with chips, delicious with bean burritos, served with tacos, added to guacamole . . . you name it.

Tomatillos—green Mexican husk tomatoes—can be bought in food stores that carry Mexican foods. Check page 128 for mail order sources of hard-to-find Mexican foods.

Chop each ingredient by hand. Or chop each ingredient separately in a food processor fitted with a steel blade. Combine the ingredients, taste, and adjust the seasonings. Allow to stand for at least 30 minutes to allow the flavors to blend. Stir well before serving.

Yield: Approximately 1¼ cups

Jack Frost Salsa

2 green tomatoes, cut in wedges
3–4 jalapeños, seeded
¼ cup diced onion
1 tablespoon chopped fresh basil
1 tablespoon red wine vinegar
Salt
Really Hot Pepper Sauce (page 30)
  or Louisiana Hot Sauce

This recipe was developed for gardeners, particularly northern growers, who inevitably lose some of their tomatoes to frost. You can beat the frost by harvesting green tomatoes and using them in salsas. Although green tomatoes have less flavor than tomatillos, or Mexican green tomatoes, they make an adequate substitute. The addition of fresh basil in this salsa is highly irregular, but very pleasant.

In a food processor fitted with a steel blade, combine the tomatoes, jalapeños, onion, and basil. Process until finely chopped and well mixed. If you do not have a food processor, finely chop the ingredients and mix by hand.

Add the vinegar, salt, and Hot Pepper Sauce to taste. Let stand for about 1 hour to allow the flavors to develop. Stir well before serving.

Yield: Approximately 1½ cups

COOKED SALSAS

Jalapeño Salsa

1 tablespoon olive oil
¾ **cup chopped jalapeños**
2 **garlic cloves, minced**
¼ **cup chopped onion**
3 **cups peeled, seeded,**
   chopped tomatoes
1 **tablespoon red wine vinegar**
1 **tablespoon chopped fresh cilantro**
1 **tablespoon chopped green olives**
Salt

This sauce is nicely hot. If you'd like to make a milder salsa, substitute sweet green bell peppers for some of the jalapeños.

In a medium-size skillet, heat the oil. Add the jalapeños, garlic, and onion. Sauté until the onion is soft, but not browned, 3–5 minutes. Add the tomatoes and cook until the tomatoes are quite soft, about 5 minutes. Add the remaining ingredients and cook for a few minutes more to give the flavors a chance to blend. Add salt to taste if it is needed. Let the salsa stand for at least 30 minutes. Stir well before serving.

Yield: Approximately 2 cups

Columbian-style Salsa Fria

1 tablespoon butter
1 teaspoon ground cumin
¼ cup diced onion
½ cup diced fresh hot pepper
2 cups chopped fresh tomatoes or
  1 (1-pound) can peeled tomatoes
¾ cup crushed unsweetened
  pineapple
¼ cup lime juice
⅛ teaspoon ground cinnamon
Salt and pepper

Pineapple gives this salsa a sweet flavor. It is a great salsa to serve with grilled fish.

In a saucepan, melt the butter. Add the cumin, onion, and hot pepper. Sauté until the onion is translucent, 2–3 minutes. Add the tomatoes, pineapple, lime juice, and cinnamon. Simmer for 30 minutes. Season to taste with salt and pepper. Cool. Serve at room temperature.

Yield: 2½ cups

Mild Red Chile Chipotle Salsa

4 chipotle chiles (no substitutes)
1 cup boiling water
1 tablespoon oil
¾ cup diced onion
¾ cup diced sweet green pepper
2–3 fresh jalapeños, diced
2 cups peeled diced ripe tomatoes or
   1 (1-pound) can peeled tomatoes
½ teaspoon dried oregano

A mild (to some) smoky salsa. Chipotle chiles are smoke-dried jalapeños. They are hot, flavorful, and there are no substitutes for them. The variation given below is a hot one. This salsa adds lots of flavor to cooked dishes, particularly barbecues. It is one of my favorite salsas for chips, and it makes a great dip when combined with sour cream.

Combine the chiles and boiling water in a nonaluminum bowl and let soak for at least 30 minutes. Remove the stems and seeds and chop.

In a nonaluminum saucepan, heat the oil and sauté the onion, sweet pepper, and jalapeños until the onion is slightly tender, 1–2 minutes. Add the chiles, soaking water, tomatoes, and oregano and remove from the heat. Process briefly in a blender or food processor until the ingredients are well mixed but still somewhat chunky.

Store extra salsa in a tightly sealed jar in the refrigerator.

Yield: 3–3½ cups

Variation

Hot Red Chile Chipotle Salsa. Make the salsa as above, but do not add the soaking water to the salsa. The yield will be reduced to approximately 2½ cups and the flavor will be *much* hotter.

Enchilada Salsa Borracha

3 tablespoons butter
4 garlic cloves, minced
4 tablespoons chile powder
3–4 jalapeños, diced
2 cups peeled diced tomatoes or
   1 (1-pound) can peeled tomatoes
2 tablespoons tomato paste
½ cup beer

A smooth, somewhat heavy sauce that is excellent with enchiladas.

In a nonaluminum saucepan, melt the butter over medium low heat. Add the garlic, chile powder, and jalapeños. Sauté until the chile powder foams, about 5 minutes. Add the remaining ingredients and bring to a boil. Simmer for 5 minutes. Then remove from the heat.

Yield: Approximately 3 cups

Tomatillo and Chile Chipotle Salsa

3 chipotle chiles
1 cup boiling water
1 tablespoon butter
1 garlic clove, minced
½ cup diced onion
1 (13-ounce) can tomatillos, drained

This salsa is very hot and very distinctively flavored. It is a great salsa with chips and delicious on quesadillas (page 122). If the flavor of this salsa knocks you out, but the heat is too much for you, you can dilute the salsa with about ⅓ cup of sour cream.

Combine the chiles and boiling water in a nonaluminum bowl. Let soak for 1 hour. Drain. Remove the stems. Chop finely.

In a nonaluminum saucepan, melt the butter. Briefly sauté the garlic and chiles until soft, 1–3 minutes. Combine the chiles, onion, and tomatillos in a food processor or blender and process until *just* mixed but still chunky. Stir well before serving.

Yield: 1 cup

Little Chicago Salsa

2 cups dried chile de arbol or any
   small hot dried chile
8 cups boiling water
2 tablespoons oil
8 garlic cloves, chopped
2 onions, chopped
4 fresh jalapeños, chopped
1½ tablespoons ground cumin
2 (1-pound) cans peeled tomatoes
2 teaspoons dried oregano
1 tablespoon sugar
1 teaspoon salt
2 cups white vinegar

This is my "house salsa." I live on Little Chicago Road, hence the name. I make up the salsa in fairly large quantities and can the extra in pint or half-pint jars. You can cut the recipe in half if you don't want to bother with canning. Unfortunately, this salsa does not freeze well. It will keep for several weeks in the refrigerator — if it isn't all eaten before then. I use this salsa in a lot of dishes. It is a thin, concentrated, richly flavored hot sauce.

The best chile to use in this salsa is dried chile de arbol, but any small hot dried chile will do. In fact, you will often find chiles labeled "small hot chiles." These may or may not be chile de arbol — but they will do the job just fine.

Combine the chiles and boiling water in a nonaluminum bowl and let soak for 1 hour.

In a large nonaluminum saucepan, heat the oil. Add the garlic, onions, jalapeños, and cumin. Sauté until the onions are just translucent, 2–3 minutes. Add the remaining ingredients, including the chiles and soaking water. Bring to a boil, partially cover with the pan lid, and simmer for about 2 hours, until the sauce has slightly thickened and the vegetables are quite soft.

Briefly process in a blender or food processor until the vegetables are pureed. The sauce will not be entirely smooth. You can strain the sauce through a nonaluminum metal strainer, but it is not necessary.

To can the salsa for long-term storage, reheat the salsa. Ladle the salsa into clean, hot pint or half-pint canning jars, leaving ½ inch head space. Seal. Process in a boiling water bath for 15 minutes. Adjust the seals if necessary. Let cool undisturbed for 12 hours. Store in a cool, dry place. Once the jars have been opened, store in the refrigerator. Shake well before using.

Yield: 4 cups

Really Hot Pepper Sauce

2 cups small hot chiles
  (chile de arbol, pasillas, etc.)
3 cups boiling water
1 tablespoon vegetable oil
6 garlic cloves, minced
2 teaspoons ground cumin
2 teaspoons dried oregano
1½ cups distilled white vinegar
1 teaspoon salt
⅛ teaspoon liquid smoke (optional)

No kidding. This one is hot. If you have a shaker bottle from a commercial hot sauce, such as Tabasco or Frank's Louisiana Red Hot Sauce, you may want to store and serve this sauce in the shaker bottle, so only a drop pours out at a time.

Combine the chiles and boiling water in a nonaluminum bowl and set aside to soak for 1 hour.

In a nonaluminum saucepan, heat the oil. Add the garlic, cumin, and oregano and sauté for 3 minutes. Add the chiles, soaking water, vinegar, and salt. Bring to a boil, then simmer, covered, for 2½ hours. Add more water, if necessary; the chiles should be just covered by the water.

When the chiles are quite soft, puree in a blender or food processor fitted with a steel blade. Strain through a nonaluminum strainer. If desired, stir in the liquid smoke.

Cover tightly and store in the refrigerator.
The sauce will keep for several months.

Yield: 1-1¼ cups

Mild Hot Pepper Sauce

2 chile chipotle
5 chile cascabel
2 chile mulato
10 chile de arbol
5 pasillas chiles
4 cups boiling water
2 tablespoons vegetable oil
6 garlic cloves, minced
1 onion, chopped
1 tablespoon dried oregano
1 tablespoon sugar
2½ cups cider vinegar
2 cups chopped tomatoes
  or 1 (1-pound) can tomatoes
2 teaspoons salt or to taste

This hot pepper sauce gives the flavor of chiles, without the overwhelming hotness of commercial sauces, such as Frank's Louisiana Red Hot Sauce or Tabasco sauce. Use it to add spice to cooked meat, fish, fowl, or eggs, and as a substitute for Tabasco sauce.

I use a variety of chiles in this sauce, but you can use whatever you have on hand. The flavor will be different, but the recipe will work.

Combine the chiles and the boiling water in a large bowl. Allow to soak for at least 1 hour. Then remove the seeds and stems from the chiles.

In a large nonaluminum saucepan, heat the oil. Add the garlic and onion and sauté until the onion is transparent and limp, 2–3 minutes. Add the remaining ingredients, including the chiles and the soaking water.

Bring to a boil and simmer, with the lid askew, for about 3 hours. The chiles should be very soft.

In a blender or a food processor fitted with a steel blade, puree the sauce. You will have to do this in two stages. Return the sauce to the pot and adjust the seasonings to taste.

For long-term storage, pour the hot sauce into clean hot half-pint or pint canning jars, leaving ¼ inch head space. Seal. Process in a boiling water bath for 15 minutes. Adjust seals if necessary. Cool undisturbed for 12 hours. Then store in a cool, dry place. If you don't want to bother with canning the sauce, you can store it in a glass jar in the refrigerator for a month or more.

Yield: 5 half-pints

Barbecue Sauce

6 chipotle chiles
1 cup boiling water
2 tablespoons butter
1 onion, diced
4 garlic cloves, minced
1½ teaspoons cumin
1½ teaspoons ground thyme
1 (12-ounce) can tomato paste
½ cup brown sugar
1½ cups cider vinegar
1½ teaspoons dry mustard
1½ cups water
1 tablespoon soy sauce
1 teaspoon Really Hot Pepper Sauce
   (page 30) or Tabasco sauce

Combine the chiles and boiling water. Soak for 1 hour. Then remove the stems and seeds and chop.

In a large nonaluminum saucepan, melt the butter. Sauté the onion, garlic, cumin, and thyme over low heat until the onions are soft and translucent, about 5 minutes. Add the chiles, soaking water, and remaining ingredients. Bring to a boil. Partially cover and simmer for 1 hour. Taste and adjust the seasonings.

This sauce can be stored in the refrigerator for at least 3 weeks. It freezes well.

Yield: About 5 cups

Louisiana Red Sauce

¼ cup butter
1 tablespoon chili powder
2 garlic cloves, minced
½ cup chopped onion
½ cup chopped green pepper
½ cup chopped celery,
   including celery leaves
2 fresh hot peppers, chopped
1 (28-ounce) can crushed
   Italian tomatoes in heavy puree
3 bay leaves
1½ teaspoons thyme
¼ teaspoon black pepper
Salt
Really Hot Sauce (page 30)
   or Tabasco sauce

This rich table sauce is a product of Creole influences. It is hot, rich, and delicious—particularly with fish, chicken, and meats. It is also excellent on rice.

In a nonaluminum saucepan, melt the butter. Add the chili powder and cook over low heat until the chili powder foams, about 2 minutes. Add the garlic, onion, green pepper, celery, and hot peppers. Sauté over medium heat until the vegetables are soft, 4–5 minutes. Add the tomatoes, bay leaves, thyme, and black pepper. Bring to a boil, then simmer for 30 minutes to blend the flavors. Taste and adjust seasonings. Serve hot or at room temperature. This sauce freezes well.

Yield: Approximately 3 cups

Harissa Sauce

2 sweet red peppers
4–5 fresh hot peppers
1 tablespoon butter
1 teaspoon ground coriander
1½ teaspoons ground cumin
1 (28-ounce) can Italian plum
   tomatoes
1 tablespoon lemon juice
3 tablespoons chopped fresh parsley
Salt

This salsa comes from North Africa. It is traditionally served with couscous. It is also great on rice—or served with chips. It goes very well with meats and chicken. I like to pour it over chicken and bake it, as in Red Pepper Chicken (page 82).

Roast the peppers by placing them under the broiler and broiling them until the skin blisters. Keep turning the peppers and broil for about 3 minutes per side. Then place the peppers in a paper bag and allow them to steam for about 10 minutes to loosen the skins. Remove from the bag, peel away the skins, and remove the seeds. Mince the peppers finely.

Melt the butter in a nonaluminum saucepan. Over low heat, sauté the peppers, coriander, and cumin until the peppers are softened, about 5 minutes. Add the tomatoes and lemon juice and simmer briefly to blend the flavors, 5-10 minutes. Stir in the parsley. Add salt to taste. Serve hot or at room temperature. This sauce will keep for at least 1 week in the refrigerator. It freezes well.

Yield: Approximately 4 cups

Hot Sesame Salsa

5 tablespoons sesame oil
1 cup chopped onions
1 cup chopped fresh hot peppers
  with seeds
6 garlic cloves, minced
16 cups chopped tomatoes
  (about 6 pounds)
1 tablespoon crushed red peppers
  (optional)
½ cup rice wine vinegar
1 teaspoon salt

If the Chinese had invented salsa, it might have tasted like this—flavored with smoky sesame oil and spicy hot. These is no end to the uses for this hot sauce. Use it as a dipping sauce for eggrolls or as a sauce base for stir fries. I like it on top of rice.

Because I use this sauce so often, I make it in quantity and can or freeze the extra sauce. You can, of course, cut the recipe in half to make about 5 cups and store the extra in the refrigerator; it will keep for several weeks or more.

In a large nonaluminum saucepan, heat the oil. Add the onions, hot peppers, and garlic. Sauté until the onions are translucent, 2–3 minutes. Add the tomatoes, cover, and cook until the tomatoes are soft and easily broken up with a spoon, 10–20 minutes. Stir occasionally.

In a blender or food processor fitted with a steel blade, process the vegetables briefly. The sauce should still be slightly chunky.

Return the sauce to the pan. Add the remaining ingredients and simmer for 10 minutes. Taste and adjust the seasoning.

For long-term storage, ladle the hot sauce into clean hot pint jars, leaving ¼ inch head space. Seal. Process in a boiling water bath for 15 minutes. Adjust the seals if necessary. Cool undisturbed for 12 hours. Store in a cool, dry place. Keep refrigerated once opened.

Yield: 5 pints

Vegetable Salsa

2 tablespoons vegetable oil
1 cup diced onions
1 cup diced celery
1 cup sliced carrots
3 garlic cloves, minced
1–2 cups chopped seeded hot
    peppers
3 tablespoons chopped fresh parsley
    or 1 tablespoon dried
1 tablespoon fresh or dried cilantro
    (optional)
4 cups tomato puree
    or canned tomatoes
    or 6 cups fresh tomatoes,
    seeded and finely chopped
½ cup wine vinegar
1 teaspoon salt
1 teaspoon sugar

This is *not* a classic salsa, but it happens to be a favorite in my house. The addition of vegetables gives it a thick texture, which makes it an excellent sandwich spread — perfect on grilled cheese sandwiches and burgers of all kinds. It is also great in omelets, on cooked rice or vegetables, and in sauces as a seasoning base. In fact, this salsa has more uses than I can list. So I make it up in double and triple batches, and put the extra up in canning jars. It freezes well.

In a large saucepan, heat the oil. Add the onions, celery, carrots, garlic, and hot peppers. Sauté until the vegetables are soft, about 10 minutes. Add the parsley, cilantro, tomatoes, vinegar, salt, and sugar. Simmer for 45 minutes.

Allow to cool slightly. Then blend to a smooth puree in a food processor or blender. You will have to do this step in at least 2 batches. Return the pureed sauce to the saucepan and simmer for another 30 minutes. Taste and adjust seasonings if necessary.

The salsa will keep in the refrigerator for a few weeks.

For long-term storage, ladle the sauce into clean hot pint or half-pint canning jars, leaving ¼ inch head space. Seal. Process in a boiling water bath for 15 minutes. Adjust seals if necessary. Allow to cool undisturbed for 24 hours. Store the jars in a cool, dry place. Once opened, the jars will keep in the refrigerator for several weeks.

Yield: 2½ pints

Red Sauce

6 ancho chiles*or
   3 cups dried red chiles
3 cups boiling water
3½–4 cups thin tomato puree
   or juice
3 garlic cloves, minced
½ cup white vinegar
1 cup water
1 teaspoon salt
3 tablespoons sugar
1 tablespoon prepared horseradish

Combine the chiles and boiling water and let soak for 30 minutes. Remove from the water. Remove the stems and seeds from the chiles and chop finely.

In a large nonaluminum saucepan, combine the chiles, tomato puree, garlic, vinegar, 1 cup water, salt, and sugar. Bring to a boil and simmer for 30 minutes. Cool slightly and process in a blender until smooth. Add the horseradish. Taste and adjust the seasonings.

This sauce will keep in the refrigerator for several weeks. For long-term storage, ladle the hot sauce into clean hot pint or half-pint canning jars, leaving ½ inch head space. Seal. Process in a boiling water bath for 15 minutes. Adjust seals if necessary. Cool undisturbed for 12 hours. Store in a cool, dry place.

* For a medium-hot sauce

Yield: Approximately 5 cups

3.
SALSA STARTERS

Salsa dishes can start a meal off with a wonderful glow. The dishes can be as simple as corn chips and an unadorned salsa for dipping, or as fancy as stuffed mushrooms.

A crudité platter of bite-size raw vegetables is delicious with a salsa sour cream dip. Carrot and celery sticks, sweet green and red pepper strips, cauliflorets, and broccoli florets are all excellent choices for the crudité platter.

No recipe is needed for chips and dip. Serve the salsa of your choice with corn chips or combine the salsa with some sour cream to make a milder dip. The proportions of salsa to sour cream are whatever tastes good to you.

Homemade chips will taste better than packaged chips. You can make homemade chips by cutting corn tortillas (the soft corn tortillas you find wrapped in the refrigerated section of your supermarket) into strips with a pair of kitchen scissors. Deep fry the strips in oil preheated to 350° F. for a minute or two until golden. Fry just a few chips at a time and watch to be sure that the oil doesn't become too hot and scorch the chips. Burnt chips will have a bitter flavor. Drain the chips well on paper bags or paper towels and serve warm.

If you want to get more elaborate, make nachos. Arrange tortilla chips on a baking dish. Top with strips of fresh or pickled chiles, then spoon on the salsa of your choice. Sprinkle a generous amount of grated cheese on top. Monterey jack cheese is traditional; but cheddar or Gruyère cheese are both excellent. Place under a broiler, about 4–6 inches from the flame and broil until the cheese melts, about 4 minutes.

Salsas can be added to soups to great advantage as well. Bean soups, hearty vegetable soups, even minestrone soup, all are made more interesting and flavorful with the addition of salsa, particularly Vegetable Salsa (page 40) and Little Chicago Salsa (page 28). I have included just 2 soups here, but I recommend you experiment further, using salsas as seasoning bases.

Guacamole

1 medium-size onion, quartered
4 garlic cloves
1 tomato, quartered
2 avocados, sliced
Juice of 1 lemon
3–4 tablespoons Little Chicago Salsa
  (page 28)
Salt

Guacamole can be served as an appetizer with chips or on a generous bed of shredded lettuce and sliced tomatoes to make a satisfying main dish salad.

In a food processor fitted with a steel blade, combine the onion, garlic, and tomato. Process until finely chopped. Add the avocado and process briefly until well mixed, but still somewhat chunky. Transfer to a nonmetal bowl. Stir in the lemon juice, salsa, and salt to taste. Allow to rest for 5–10 minutes to allow the flavors to blend, or cover tightly and store in the refrigerator. Storing the guacamole with the avocado pit in the bowl is said to prevent browning. Stir well before serving.

Yield: Approximately 2 cups

Little Chicago Eggrolls

6 cups thinly sliced or grated Chinese or green cabbage or bok choy or a combination of each
1 teaspoon salt
1 cup cooked shredded turkey or chicken or baby shrimp
¼ cup Little Chicago Salsa (page 28)
½ cup chopped scallions, including green tops
1 cup grated carrots
1 cup fresh or frozen peas or snow peas
2 teaspoons sesame oil
Oil for deep frying
Flour
Approximately 12 eggroll skins
1 egg white

The salsa in these eggrolls adds a little extra punch and a lot of extra flavor. I usually serve eggrolls with salsa, a sweet and sour plum sauce, and mustard sauce on the side. The mustard and salsa together make a powerful combination. To make a mustard sauce, combine a few tablespoons of dry mustard powder with enough water to get a good spooning consistency.

First, prepare the filling by combining the cabbage and salt in a colander. Weight with a heavy plate and set aside to drain for about 30 minutes. In a small bowl, combine the turkey and salsa and set aside for about 30 minutes.

Squeeze out any excess moisture from the cabbage. In a large bowl, combine the cabbage, turkey and salsa, scallions, carrots, peas, and sesame oil. Mix well. Taste and adjust the seasonings. The filling should taste somewhat salty and spicy. You can hold the filling in the refrigerator for up to several hours, if desired.

In a deep heavy saucepan or deep fryer, begin to heat the oil for deep frying.

On a lightly floured board or tray, roll the eggrolls. Lay an eggroll skin on the board with 1 corner pointing toward you. Using a slotted spoon, scoop ¼–½ cup of filling onto the center of the eggroll skin. Bring the corner nearest you up over the filling. Tuck the skin over the filling, compressing the filling into a log. Bring in both side corners, folding over the filling. They will not meet in the middle. Now roll the eggroll. Keep tucking in the sides of the skin and coaxing the filling into the log shape. Brush the last corner with the egg white and seal. Place the eggroll on a floured baking sheet, seam side up. Roll the eggroll in additional flour if the wrapper seems at all wet. Add more flour

to the rolling surface, if needed, and continue rolling eggrolls until all the filling has been used. Try to avoid the liquid that accumulates in the bottom of the bowl of filling.

It is best to fry the eggrolls as soon as they have been rolled, but they can be held for up to an hour if they are well floured.

When the oil temperature reaches about 365° F., it is ready for frying. Carefully place about 3 eggrolls at a time in the oil and fry until golden, about 3 minutes. Remove from the oil and drain in an upright position. Drain for just a few minutes. Serve hot.

Yield: About 12 eggrolls

Cold Sesame Salsa Noodles

½ **pound Chinese rice vermicelli noodles or very thin spaghetti, such as cappellini (angel hair)**
3 **tablespoons sesame oil**
¼ **cup tahini (sesame paste)**
2 **tablespoons tamari or soy sauce**
5 **tablespoons Hot Sesame Salsa (page 38)**
2 **teaspoons rice vinegar**
2 **teaspoons water**
3 **garlic cloves, minced**
2 **cups fresh or frozen peas (optional)**
4 **tablespoons chopped scallions, including some green tops**

These cold noodles make a wonderful first course for a Chinese meal. With the addition of peas, these noodles also make an excellent light lunch or supper.

Rice vermicelli noodles are available at Oriental markets. You could also substitute cellophane noodles, which are made from mung beans.

Prepare the noodles according to the package directions. Drain. Toss with the sesame oil and refrigerate until well chilled, at least 1 hour.

Just before serving, whisk together the tahini, tamari, salsa, vinegar, water, and garlic. Pour over the noodles and toss to coat the noodles with the dressing. Add the peas, if desired. Frozen peas will defrost by the time the noodles are served. Fresh peas can be steamed for 2 minutes, then refreshed in cold water and drained before they are added to the dish. Or they can be tossed in raw. Add 3 tablespoons of the scallions. Toss to mix well. Serve with the remaining 1 tablespoon of scallions garnishing the top.

Yield: 4–6 servings

Pork Empanadas

2 pounds pork butt or shoulder roast
1 onion, quartered
2 garlic cloves
½ teaspoon salt
1 teaspoon dried oregano
1 teaspoon ground cumin
2 bay leaves
1½ cups plus 2 tablespoons
  all-purpose flour
¾ cup Masa Harina
1 teaspoon baking powder
¼ teaspoon salt
½ cup solid vegetable shortening
  or lard
1 egg, beaten
½ cup milk
Really Hot Pepper Sauce (page 30)
1 cup Mild or Hot Red Chile Chipotle Salsa (pages 24-25)
½ teaspoon salt
Milk

Empanadas are Mexican turnovers. These tasty morsels can be served as appetizers, packed into brown bags or picnic baskets for lunch, or snacked on at any time.

This recipe is not as complicated as it may look on first glance. The pork filling is easy to make and can be used with other dishes, such as tacos. The dough is as easy to make and roll out as pie dough.

Place the pork in a large pot. Cover with water. Add the onion, garlic, ½ teaspoon salt, oregano, cumin, and bay leaves. Bring to a boil, reduce the heat, and simmer for 1½ hours.

While the pork cooks, prepare the dough. Sift together the flour, Masa Harina, baking powder, and ¼ teaspoon salt. In a separate bowl, beat together the egg and ½ cup milk. Make a well in the center of the dry ingredients. Add the egg mixture and stir with a fork until the dough comes together in a ball. Divide the dough into 16 even-size pieces and roll each piece into a ball. Place in a bowl, cover, and refrigerate.

After the pork has simmered for 1½ hours, preheat the oven to 375° F. Remove the pork from the liquid, saving the liquid for soup stock. Place the pork in a baking dish or Dutch oven. Brush with the Hot Pepper Sauce. Bake for 45–60 minutes, until the meat shreds easily with a fork. Remove the meat from the oven and shred it into small pieces. Combine with the Red Chile Chipotle Salsa and the remaining ½ teaspoon salt.

On a lightly floured surface, flatten a piece of dough with the palm of your hand. With a rolling pin, roll out the dough to make a 5-inch circle, about ⅛ inch thick. Place 2–3 tablespoons of filling in the center of the dough. Brush the edges of the dough with milk. Fold the dough over the filling to make a half circle. Pinch the edges together. Press the tines of a fork around the sealed edges. Place on a lightly greased baking sheet. Continue rolling and filling until all the dough and filling is used. Bake for 20 minutes, until golden. Remove to a rack and cool for about 5 minutes. Serve warm.

You can freeze these — baked or unbaked. To bake frozen empanadas, do not thaw. Place the frozen empanadas on a lightly greased baking sheet. Place in a preheated 350° F. oven and bake for 25–30 minutes, until golden. Reheat baked frozen empanadas at 350° F. for 15–20 minutes.

Yield: 16 empanadas

Spinach Cheese Empanadas

1½ cups plus 2 tablespoons
  all-purpose flour
¾ cup Masa Harina
1 teaspoon baking powder
¼ teaspoon salt
½ cup solid vegetable shortening
  or lard
1 egg, beaten
½ cup milk
10 cups raw spinach
  (about 2 cups cooked)
2 cups crumbled feta cheese
  (8 ounces)
1 cup grated jack cheese
½ onion, diced
1 cup Jalapeño Salsa (page 22)
Milk

Sift together the flour, Masa Harina, baking powder, and salt. Cut in the shortening until the mixture resembles coarse crumbs. Beat together the egg and ½ cup milk. Make a well in the center of the dry ingredients and pour in the egg mixture. Stir with a fork until the dough comes together in a ball. Divide the ball into 16 even-size pieces and roll each into a ball. Cover and refrigerate for at least 30 minutes.

While the dough rests, prepare the filling. Steam the spinach over boiling water until wilted, 3–4 minutes. Drain. Cool. Squeeze out as much excess water as possible.

Combine the spinach with the feta and jack cheeses. Add the onion and salsa. Mix well. Taste and adjust the seasoning.

Preheat the oven to 350° F.

On a lightly floured surface, flatten 1

dough ball with the palm of your hand. With a rolling pin, roll out the dough to a 5-inch circle, about ⅛ inch thick. Place 2–3 tablespoons of filling in the center of the circle. Brush the edges of the dough with milk. Fold the dough over the filling to form a half circle. Pinch the edges together. Press the tines of a fork around the sealed edges. Place on a lightly greased baking sheet. Continue rolling and filling until all the dough and filling is used. Bake for 20 minutes, until golden. Remove to a rack to cool for 5 minutes. Serve warm.

Extra empanadas can be frozen baked or unbaked. To bake frozen empanadas, do not thaw. Place the frozen empanadas on a lightly greased baking sheet. Place in a preheated 350° F. oven and bake for 25–30 minutes, until golden. Reheat baked frozen empanadas at 350° F. for 15–20 minutes.

Yield: 16 empanadas

Stuffed Mushrooms

1 pound mushrooms
1 onion
2 garlic cloves
3 tablespoons butter
1 cup grated Parmesan cheese
6 tablespoons Vegetable Salsa
   (page 40)
½ cup bread crumbs
Oil

The salsa gives flavor but not too much hotness. Make the mushrooms in advance and heat them when you are ready to serve. Serve these as party hor d'oeuvres or appetizers. They won't require a warning for those who don't appreciate hot foods.

Wash the mushrooms and pat dry. Break off the stems and set the caps aside. Mince the mushroom stems. A food processor does this job well.

Mince the onion and garlic. Again, the food processor does this job well. (Do not process the onion and mushrooms together.)

Melt the butter in a sauté pan over medium low heat. Add the onion and garlic and simmer for 3–4 minutes, until the onion is quite soft. Add the mushrooms and continue to simmer, stirring frequently for another 3 minutes. Remove from the heat.

Combine the mushroom/onion mixture with the cheese, salsa, and bread crumbs. Brush the mushroom caps with oil and fill with 1–2 tablespoons of filling. Place the mushrooms in a greased baking dish. Hold in the refrigerator until you are ready to serve.

Just before serving, place the mushrooms under a preheated broiler and broil for 4–5 minutes until the tops are browned. Serve hot.

Yield: 6 servings

Salsa Hush Puppies

1½ cups cornmeal
½ cup all-purpose unbleached flour
1 tablespoon baking powder
1 teaspoon salt
2 eggs
1 cup milk
1 cup Salsa Cruda (page 16),
   Jalapeño Salsa (page 22),
   Pickled Pepper Salsa (page 18),
   or Jack Frost Salsa (page 21)
½ cup finely chopped jalapeños
   (optional)
Oil for deep frying

Sift together the cornmeal, flour, baking powder, and salt. In another bowl, beat the eggs. Add the milk, salsa, and jalapeños. Add to the cornmeal mixture. Stir until just mixed. The batter will be slightly lumpy.

Heat the oil for deep frying to 350° F. Drop the batter by the tablespoon into the hot fat. Fry until golden, about 5 minutes. If necessary, turn the hush puppies over as they fry to be sure they brown evenly. Drain well. Serve at once.

Yield: 4 servings

Garden Salsa Soup

6 cups chicken or vegetable stock
6 cups peeled, seeded,
  and chopped tomatoes
½ pound uncooked vermicelli
4 cups mixed diced fresh or frozen
  vegetables (celery, corn, zucchini,
  peas, snap beans)
4–5 tablespoons Little Chicago Salsa
  (page 28)
Salt
½ cup chopped chives or scallions
Sour cream or yogurt

In a soup pot, combine the stock and tomatoes. Bring to a boil. Add the vermicelli, breaking it up as you add it to the boiling liquid. Stir once or twice to separate the vermicelli. Boil for 5–7 minutes, until the vermicelli is just tender. Do not overcook.

Add the vegetables and salsa, reduce the heat, and simmer for about 3 minutes, until the vegetables are barely tender. Season to taste with salt, if it is needed. Remove from the heat and stir in the chives or scallions. Serve immediately.

Pass a bowl of sour cream or yogurt at the table for those who find the soup too spicy.

Yield: 6 servings

Gazpacho

1 cup Avocado Salsa Cruda
  (page 19), Salsa Cruda (page 16),
  or Pickled Pepper Salsa (page 18)
2 cups grated cucumbers
  (pickling cucumbers are
  recommended, no need
  to peel them)
4 cups tomato juice
Really Hot Pepper Sauce (page 30)
  or a Tabasco-type sauce (optional)
Salt

With extra salsa on hand, you can make Gazpacho in minutes. It's a very cool and refreshing chilled soup for a hot day. Pass a bowl of corn chips with the soup.

In a large nonaluminum bowl, combine the salsa, cucumbers, and tomato juice. Add the hot sauce and salt to taste. Chill well. Serve over ice.

For a very fancy presentation, freeze ice cubes with a parsley or cilantro leaf in each cube.

Yield: 4 servings

4.

SALADS

It takes a hearty salad to stand up to the strong flavors of a salsa, and the salads gathered here are quite hearty. In fact, the pasta salads can be served as a meal by themselves. There are many other combinations of salads that work well with salsas — rice salads and different combinations of pasta salads among others.

Little Chicago Potato Salad

4 medium-size potatoes, cubed
  (peeling is optional)
2 tablespoons safflower oil
2 tablespoons red wine vinegar
¼ cup Little Chicago Salsa (page 28)
¾ teaspoon salt
1 celery rib, diced
1 carrot, grated
1 sweet green bell pepper, diced
¼ cup chopped fresh chives
½ cup mayonnaise
⅛ teaspoon ground thyme
Salt and pepper

If you like potato salad, and you like piquant foods, you'll probably want to double or triple this recipe.

Boil the potatoes in water to cover until tender, but not mushy, 5–8 minutes. Drain well.

In a large salad bowl, combine the oil, vinegar, salsa, and ¾ teaspoon salt. Add the warm potatoes and toss to coat well. Cover and refrigerate for 2–8 hours. Stir occasionally.

Add the remaining ingredients to the potatoes. Mix well. Season to taste with salt and pepper. Serve at once or chill.

Yield: 4 servings

Spicy Potato Salad

4 medium-size potatoes, cubed
  (peeling is optional)
1 cup Jalapeño Salsa (page 22)
  or Pickled Pepper Salsa (page 18)
1 teaspoon salt
1 cup diced celery
½ cup thinly sliced radishes
½ cup yogurt or more to taste
Salt

This salad doesn't keep particularly well; the dressing becomes watery. So make only as much as you will eat in one sitting. The flavor is quite hot, but the yogurt cools down the palate. Add as much as needed.

Boil the potatoes in water to cover until tender, but not mushy, 5–8 minutes. Drain well.

In a large salad bowl, combine the warm potatoes with the salsa and salt. Toss to coat well. Cover and refrigerate for 2–3 hours.

Just before serving, add the celery, radishes, and yogurt. Add more yogurt if necessary. Season to taste with salt. Serve at once.

Yield: 4 servings

Pasta Salad Verde

1 pound spinach pasta
2 tablespoons unrefined safflower
   or olive oil
1 teaspoon unrefined safflower
   or olive oil
½ cup pine nuts
2 hard-boiled eggs
¾ cup Jack Frost Salsa (page 21)
   or Tomatillo Salsa (page 20)
Salt
1 cup diced zucchini
3 scallions, chopped
2 jalapeños, diced (optional)
1 cup diced blanched
   or fresh green beans

The green spinach pasta, green salsa, and green vegetables combine for a very attractive salad. You can substitute other salsa crudas or vegetables with delicious results, but it is fun to keep the color green.

Cook the pasta according to the package directions. Drain and toss with 2 tablespoons oil. Set aside to cool.

In a small heavy skillet over medium low heat, heat 1 teaspoon oil. Add the pine nuts and lightly toast the pine nuts until golden, about 4 minutes.

With a fork, crumble the hard-boiled eggs. Combine with the salsa. Season to taste with salt.

In a large salad bowl, combine the pasta, pine nuts, vegetables, and salsa. Toss well to combine. Serve at once.

Yield: 4 servings

Seafood Pasta Salad

½ cup Barbecue Sauce (page 34)
Juice of 1 lemon
½ cup safflower oil
1 teaspoon prepared horseradish
½ teaspoon sugar
1 tablespoon chopped fresh basil
½ pound cooked crabmeat
½ pound cooked shrimp
½ pound pasta (spiral fusilli pasta is recommended)
1 cup fresh or frozen peas
1 cup julienne-sliced zucchini
1 carrot, julienne-sliced
½ green pepper, julienne-sliced
½ cup chopped black olives
Lettuce

One of my very favorite recipes.

In a large bowl, combine the Barbecue Sauce, lemon juice, oil, horseradish, sugar, and basil. Mix well. Add the crabmeat and shrimp and toss to coat with the dressing. Marinate in the refrigerator for at least 30 minutes.

While the seafood marinates, cook the pasta in plenty of boiling water until just done. Drain well and add to the seafood. Toss to coat with the dressing. Return to the refrigerator for at least 30 minutes.

Just before serving, prepare the vegetables. For the best color, blanch fresh peas in boiling salted water for 1 minute. Add frozen peas directly to the salad; they will defrost within 5 minutes. Add the zucchini, carrot, green pepper, and olives. Toss the salad to mix the vegetables with the pasta.

Serve on a platter, garnished with extra strips of carrots or zucchini if desired.

Yield: 4-6 servings

Chicken Pasta Salad

½ cup **Little Chicago Salsa** (page 28)
Juice of 4 limes (¼ cup)
½ cup **safflower oil**
1 tablespoon **grated fresh ginger root**
2½ cups **cooked shredded chicken**
  or turkey
¾ pound **rice noodles or pasta**
1 cup **diagonally sliced green beans**
1 **avocado, sliced**
1 cup **sliced radishes**
½ cup **halved cherry tomatoes**
1 cup **diagonally sliced celery**
4 **apricots or 1 cup mandarin orange**
  sections
¼–½ cup **sour cream** (optional)
Lettuce

The salsa in this salad makes it a rather spicy dish. For those timid of palate, pass a bowl of sour cream with the salad. Or mix in the sour cream just before serving. Those who like their foods spicy will find this refreshing "hot" salad a welcome change.

The rice noodles, available at Oriental food stores, make this pasta salad particularly light, perfect for a summer meal. Substitute a spaghetti, such as cappellini (angel hair) or spiral pasta, if you can't find rice noodles.

Combine the salsa, lime juice, oil, and ginger root. Mix well. Add the chicken and stir to coat. Cover and place in the refrigerator.

Prepare the noodles or pasta according to the package directions. Drain, cool, and add to the marinating chicken. Mix well to coat with the marinade and return to the refrigerator to marinate for 1–3 hours.

Blanch the green beans in boiling water to cover for about 1 minute. Drain, plunge into cold water to cool rapidly, and drain. (This blanching step is optional.) Add to the salad, along with the avocado, radishes, tomatoes, and celery. If desired, hold some vegetables in reserve to arrange on top of the salad.

Blanch the apricots in boiling water to cover for 30 seconds to loosen the skins. Remove from the water, plunge into cold water, then drain. The skins should just slide off. Slice and add to the salad. If you are using fresh mandarin oranges, simply peel and add to the salad. Canned mandarin oranges should be drained before being measured.

Toss the salad to mix in all the vegetables and fruit. Arrange on a platter. Arrange the reserved vegetables on top and serve at once.

Yield: 4 servings

Spicy Bulgur Salad

1½ cups uncooked bulgur
3 cups boiling water
2 tablespoons olive oil
1 teaspoon salt
½ cup Avocado Salsa Cruda
   (page 19), Salsa Cruda (page 16),
   or Jalapeño Salsa (page 22)
1½ cups diced cucumbers
1 cup chopped tomatoes
   (2 tomatoes)
½ cup fresh parsley leaves
1 tablespoon chopped fresh mint

This is a classic tabouli salad, with a little extra punch.

In a large bowl, combine the bulgur and boiling water. Stir well. Cover and set aside for 15 minutes. Drain, rinse with cold tap water, and drain well.

In a large salad bowl, toss the bulgur with the oil and salt. Add the remaining ingredients and toss well to mix. Taste and adjust the seasoning. Cover and refrigerate for at least 1 hour to allow the flavors to blend.

Yield: 4–6 servings

5.

SALSA BARBECUES, MAIN DISHES, AND MEXICAN DELIGHTS

In each of the recipes collected here, salsa is used as the main flavoring agent. Some of these dishes are quite hot. Some dishes are flavorful but not hot, as the effect of the salsa is mitigated by the presence of other ingredients. For those who can't taste their foods unless they are very hot, always serve a bottle of Really Hot Sauce (page 30) on the table.

Consider that the salsas recommended for each recipe are just that, recommendations. Experiment with different salsas to get flavors that please your palate.

Salsas and barbecues were particularly meant for each other. A spicy hot salsa brings out the very best flavors of meats and vegetables cooked on a grill. And the smoke flavor brings out the best in a salsa, adding richness to the flavor.

Barbecue is one of the main innovations Americans have contributed to the culinary world. With the recent upswing in the popularity of American foods comes a new popularity in barbecues — along with a lot of new styles of barbecue grills and new wisdom (or opinions).

For the recipes included here, any barbecue grill will do — from a homemade barbecue pit built from cinder blocks and an old grill, to a patio barbecue, to a new, expensive water smoker/barbecue unit.

Whatever your barbecue set up, you have to build a fire in it. Start your fire 30–60 minutes before you want to start cooking. Hard wood, if you have it available and have a grill high enough above the fire, makes a great barbecue. If you are cooking on a regular patio-style barbecue, a combination of charcoal or hardwood briquets (more expensive) and wood chips works just fine. It is a good idea to start a fire with crumpled newspaper or dry wood kindling rather than lighter fluid. While most people won't detect the slight chemical flavor the lighter fluid imparts, it is nice to avoid that kind of chemical when possible.

For extra smoky flavor, add wet wood chips to the fire. Soak the wood chips in water for about 10 minutes before setting them on the fire. Lay the wood chips on the fire just before you add the food. Mesquite wood chips are extremely popular and impart a very distinct flavor to foods. Actually any wood can be used, including grapevine cuttings, apple and other fruit woods, hickory, and maple.

The amount of time it will take to cook foods on a grill depends on the closeness of the food to the hot coals and the heat of the coals. Generally, a hot fire burns red with a low flame, a medium-hot fire has a slightly red glow, no flames, and the coals are covered with ash. The guidelines for cooking times in this chapter should be used as a guide, but let your common sense make the final decisions as to whether a dish is done or not.

Grilled Baby Zucchini

1 cup Mild Red Chile Chipotle Salsa
   (page 24)
¼ cup oil
¼ teaspoon salt
4 baby zucchini, no more than
   5 inches long

About 1 hour before serving, combine the salsa, oil, and salt in a bowl. Slice the zucchini lengthwise, about ¼ inch thick. Discard the end slices that are mainly peel. Marinate the zucchini in the salsa combination for about 1 hour.

Prepare the fire in the grill. Over medium heat, lay the zucchini on a lightly oiled grill, basting with the extra marinade. Grill, turning frequently and basting generously, until the zucchini are fork tender, about 5 minutes. Serve at once.

Yield: 4 servings

Grilled Eggplant Steaks

2 small eggplants (about
⅔ pound each)
Salt
About ½ cup Barbecue Sauce
(page 34)
Oil

These eggplant steaks make delicious sandwiches. Serve them with warm crusty Italian bread and Barbecued Skewered Vegetables (page 74). Pass feta cheese and extra Barbecue Sauce.

Peel the eggplant if desired and slice lengthwise about ½ inch thick. Sprinkle with salt and set aside to drain for about 30 minutes. Pat dry. Brush with the barbecue sauce.

Prepare the fire in the grill. Over a medium fire, lay the eggplant steaks on a lightly oiled grill. Grill for about 15 minutes, until the eggplant is tender, turning every few minutes and brushing with more barbecue sauce.

Serve hot. Pass additional barbecue sauce at the table.

Yield: 4 servings

Barbecued Skewered Vegetables

Juice of 1 lemon
¼ cup safflower oil
2 teaspoons Mild Hot Pepper Sauce
  (page 32)
2 tablespoons Barbecue Sauce
  (page 34))
¼ cup finely chopped fresh basil
2 small zucchini, cut in 1-inch slices
2 green peppers, cut in 1-inch cubes
8 tiny boiling onions

If you are generous with the marinade, splashing it onto the vegetables so some falls on the fire, you will get a delicious smoky taste. These vegetables are great in sandwiches with Grilled Eggplant (page 73) or served over rice.

Combine the lemon juice, oil, Mild Hot Pepper Sauce, Barbecue Sauce, and basil in a nonaluminum bowl. Mix well. Add the vegetables and marinate for at least 1 hour. Stir occasionally.

Prepare a medium-hot fire. Arrange the vegetables on barbecue skewers and lay on the grill. Baste frequently and generously with the remaining marinade. Turn the vegetables so they cook evenly. The vegetables should be tender, but still crispy, in about 20 minutes. Serve hot.

Yield: 4 servings

Barbecued Potatoes

**4 medium-size potatoes, peeled and
  quartered, or 8–12 new potatoes,
  peeled**
Water to cover
½ cup Barbecue Sauce (page 34)
¼ cup safflower oil
½ teaspoon salt
**About 8 sprigs of fresh basil
  (optional)**

Parboil the potatoes in water to cover until *slightly* tender, about 8 minutes. Drain.

Combine the barbecue sauce, oil, and salt in a large bowl. Add the hot potatoes and set aside to marinate for 1–3 hours.

Prepare the fire in the grill.

Arrange the potatoes on barbecue skewers. Moisten the basil leaves with water. Lay the basil over the hot barbecue coals. Lay the potatoes on the grill and cook for about 5 minutes per side, basting as you turn the potatoes with the extra marinade. The potatoes are ready when they are fork tender. This should take about 20 minutes. If the coals are hot enough, the potatoes will have a crispy barbecue coating on the outside. Over medium or low coals, the crispy skin will not develop — either way the potatoes are delicious.

Yield: 4 servings

Corn and Pepper Packets

3 ears fresh sweet corn
2 tablespoons butter
2 garlic cloves, minced
½ sweet green pepper, diced
½ sweet red pepper, diced
½ cup Barbecue Sauce (page 34)
  or Mild Red Chile Chipotle Salsa
  (page 24)
3 sprigs fresh basil

With a sharp paring knife, strip the kernels from the corn cob. Set aside in a bowl.

In a sauté pan, melt the butter. Add the garlic and peppers and sauté until the peppers are well coated with butter and just beginning to soften, about 2 minutes. Remove from the heat and combine with the corn, being sure to include all the butter. Add the sauce and mix well.

Cut 3 squares of aluminum foil, about 8 inches each. Place a third of the vegetables on each foil square. Place a sprig of fresh basil on top of each vegetable packet. Fold the aluminum foil in a butcher's fold.

Place the foil packets on the grill, seam side up, and cook for 20–30 minutes, depending on how hot the fire is and hot close the packets are to the coals. Serve directly from the foil packets, or empty the packets onto serving plates.

Yield: 3 servings

Grilled Swordfish

2 pounds swordfish steaks,
  cut about 1½ inches thick
1 cup Red Sauce (page 42)
¼ cup oil
Juice of 1 lemon

Rinse the fish and pat dry. In a shallow bowl or baking dish, combine the sauce, oil, and lemon juice. Add the fish, turning to coat both sides of the steaks with the sauce. Cover and refrigerate for 1 hour, turning the steaks once or twice.

Prepare the fire in the grill. Brush the grill lightly with oil. Place the steaks on the grill, 4–6 inches from the coals. Brush generously with the marinade. The marinade should spatter onto the coals; this creates smoke to flavor the fish. Baste generously every few minutes. Turn the fish one or more times to cook evenly on both sides. The fish is done when it flakes easily with the fork, in 20–30 minutes, depending on how thick the steaks are, and how hot the fire is. Serve at once, passing additional Red Sauce.

Yield: 4 servings

Grilled Trout with Vegetables

⅓ cup safflower oil
⅓ cup wine vinegar
1 garlic clove, minced
2 tablespoons Vegetable Salsa
(page 40)
½ teaspoon salt
1 onion, thinly sliced
2 small zucchini, thinly sliced
(about 3 cups)
1 green pepper, julienne-sliced
4 whole boned trout,
about ½ pound each
¾ cup Vegetable Salsa (page 40)

About 1 hour before cooking, combine the oil, vinegar, garlic, 2 tablespoons Vegetable Salsa, and salt in a medium-size bowl. Mix well. Add the onion, zucchini, and green pepper. Set aside to marinate.

Prepare the fire in the outdoor barbecue. The coals should be *very* hot before the fish is set on the grill.

To prepare the fish, rinse well and pat dry. Dip a brush in the vegetable marinade and generously brush the fish with the mixture, coating the inside and outside of the fish. Set each trout on a separate large sheet of aluminum foil. Drain off the vegetable marinade and reserve to use in a salad dressing, if desired. Divide the vegetables among the fish, spooning the vegetables inside the trout. Cover the vegetables in each fish with about 3 tablespoons of the salsa. Fold the fish over the vegetables. Wrap tightly in the aluminum foil.

Preheat the broiler or check to make sure the coals are very hot. Broil the fish in the preheated broiler or over hot coals for 12–18 minutes, until the fish flakes easily when tested with a fork. It takes longer to cook the fish on a grill then it does in the oven broiler. Remove the fish from the aluminum foil onto individual serving plates. Pour the juices from the foil packet over the fish and serve.

Yield: 4 servings

Barbecued Wings

4 pounds chicken wings
1⅓ cups Barbecue Sauce (page 34)
4 teaspoons Mild Hot Pepper Sauce
  (page 32) or 1½ teaspoons Really
  Hot Pepper Sauce (page 30)
1 tablespoon ground cumin

Chicken wings are excellent for barbecues because they take only 15–20 minutes to cook on the grill, compared to 60 minutes for chicken quarters.

There will be some barbecue sauce left over from the grilling. Serve it on the side with rice or crusty French bread.

Split the wings to separate the drumettes from the wings. Rinse and pat dry.

Combine the Barbecue Sauce, Hot Pepper Sauce, and cumin in a large nonaluminum bowl. Add the chicken and toss to coat with the sauce. Cover and marinate in the refrigerator for 5–8 hours.

Prepare the fire in the grill. Over medium hot coals, about 4 inches from the fire, lay the chicken pieces on the grill. Cook, basting and turning frequently, until the chicken is done, 15–20 minutes. Serve hot.

Yield: 4–6 servings

Barbecued Ribs

3 pounds country-style pork ribs
2 cups Red Sauce (page 42)
　or Barbecue Sauce (page 34)

Pour the sauce over the ribs and let marinate overnight, or for at least 5 hours.

Preheat the oven to 350° F. Place the ribs in a single layer in a baking dish. Pour the extra sauce over the ribs. Cover tightly with foil and bake for 1 hour.

Prepare the fire in the grill. Over medium hot coals, place the ribs on the grill, basting generously with juices from the baking dish. Grill, turning frequently and basting generously, for 15–20 minutes, until the ribs are well-done, but not dried out. Serve with extra sauce on the side.

Yield: 4 servings

Red Pepper Chicken

¾ cup flour
1 tablespoon ground cumin
1 teaspoon paprika or cayenne
1 teaspoon salt
3½ pounds chicken, cut up
2 tablespoons oil
2 cups Harissa Sauce (page 36)
¼ cup water

Serve plenty of rice to take advantage of all the delicious sauce that accompanies this chicken. Although the Harissa Sauce starts out fairly hot, the final sauce is just slightly piquant — and very rich and flavorful.

In a bowl, combine the flour, cumin, paprika, and salt. Rinse the chicken and pat dry with paper toweling. Dredge in the flour to coat well. Reserve the extra flour.

In a large Dutch oven, heat the oil. Brown the chicken on both sides, about 5 minutes per side. Drain off any excess oil. Add the sauce, cover, and simmer over low heat for 45–60 minutes. Test for doneness by pricking a drumstick. The chicken is done when the juices run clear and the flesh is very tender.

Remove the chicken to a warmed platter, leaving the cooking liquids in the pan.

Combine 2 tablespoons of the reserved flour with ¼ cup water. Stir to make a smooth paste. Bring the cooking liquids to a boil, stirring frequently to prevent scorching. Stir in the flour and cook, stirring constantly until the sauce thickens. Remove from the heat. Pour the sauce over the chicken and serve at once.

Yield: 4 servings

Red Chicken on Yellow Rice

1 pound boned and skinned chicken
  breasts, cut in 1½ inch cubes
½ cup Little Chicago Salsa (page 28)
3 tablespoons olive
  or any vegetable oil
1 cup diced onion
1 cup diced sweet green pepper
1 cup diced sweet red pepper
3 cups uncooked white rice
2 tablespoons achiote
¼ cup boiling water
1–2 teaspoons salt
5½ cups boiling water
2 cups fresh or frozen peas
1 tablespoons capers (optional)
1 cup chopped scallions,
  including green tops
1 cup sliced black olives (optional)

The flavoring of the rice comes from achiote, a paste derived from annatto seeds. It gives the rice a delicate yellow color and a very special flavor. I often make the rice, without the chicken, as an alternative to the tomato-based Spanish rice.

Combine the chicken and salsa in a non-aluminum bowl. Cover and refrigerate for 1 hour.

Heat 1 tablespoon of the oil in a large skillet. Add the chicken and salsa and cook until the chicken is tender, about 8 minutes. Return to the bowl with the salsa and cover. Refrigerate for 5–8 hours.

About 30 minutes before serving, remove the chicken from the refrigerator. If the chicken has absorbed all the salsa, add another tablespoon or so of salsa or water to prevent the chicken from drying out. Heat, covered, over very low heat while you prepare the rice.

Heat the remaining 2 tablespoons oil in a large skillet or Dutch oven. Add the onion, green pepper, red pepper, and rice. Stir to evenly coat the rice with the oil. Sauté over low heat for about 5 minutes, stirring constantly.

Crumble the achiote into a small bowl. Add ¼ cup boiling water and stir to thoroughly dissolve the achiote. Pour into the rice, and cook, stirring constantly for about 5 minutes. Stir in the salt and 5½ cups boiling water. Stir well. Cover and cook over low heat until all the liquid is absorbed, about 20 minutes.

Remove from the heat. Fluff the rice with a fork. Mix in the chicken, peas, and capers. Return the cover and allow the peas to cook for about 5 minutes. Arrange the rice on a heated platter. Top with the scallions and black olives to garnish. Serve at once.

Yield: 8–10 servings

Variation

Spiced Pork with Yellow Rice. Substitute the shredded pork filling of the Empanadas (page 50) for the chicken and salsa. Proceed with the recipe above.

Buffalo-style Chicken Wings

4 pounds chicken wings
½ cup Really Hot Pepper Sauce
    (page 30)
Oil for deep frying
3 tablespoons butter
6 garlic cloves, minced

Split the wings to separate the drumette from the wing. Rinse and pat dry. Pour the Hot Pepper Sauce over the chicken, tossing to coat each piece well. Marinate the wings in the refrigerator for up to 3 hours. The longer the wings marinate, the hotter the flavor.

When you are ready to serve, preheat the oil to 365° F. Fry the chicken, a few pieces at a time, until golden, 5–8 minutes. Drain the pieces as you remove them from the oil.

While the chicken fries, prepare a sauce by combining the butter, garlic, and hot sauce marinade in a saucepan. Heat.

To serve, place the wings on a warmed serving platter. Pour the warmed sauce over the wings. Serve at once with celery and carrot sticks and blue cheese dressing on the side.

Yield: 4–6 servings

Fettuccine Salsa Marinara

2 tablespoons olive oil
6 garlic cloves, minced
1 sweet green pepper, finely diced
1 hot pepper, finely diced (optional)
1 (28-ounce) can Italian plum
   tomatoes
4–6 tablespoons Little Chicago Salsa
   (page 28)
½ teaspoon sugar or more to taste
¼ teaspoon salt or more to taste
1 tablespoon fresh oregano leaves
   or 1 teaspoon dried
3 tablespoons chopped fresh basil
   or 1 tablespoon dried
¾–1 pound uncooked shrimp, peeled
   and deveined
1 pound fettuccine
Parmesan cheese

A loaf of crusty Italian bread is a must for mouth-cooling with this dish.

Heat the oil in a nonaluminum saucepan. Add the garlic and peppers and sauté until the peppers are soft, 3–4 minutes. Add the tomatoes, salsa, sugar, and salt. Simmer for 15 minutes. As the sauce simmers, break up the tomatoes with a spoon. Add the herbs and simmer for 5 minutes more. Taste and adjust the seasonings. Keep warm.

Heat plenty of salted water for the pasta. About 15 minutes before serving, add the shrimp to the sauce and simmer gently. Cook the fettuccine according to the package directions. Drain the pasta. Spoon the shrimp and sauce over the fettuccine and serve at once. Pass a bowl of cheese at the table.

Yield: 4 servings

Scallops in Louisiana Red Sauce

2–3 cups cooked white or brown rice
3 cups Louisiana Red Sauce
  (page 35)
2 pounds bay scallops
Really Hot Sauce (page 30)
  or Tabasco sauce
Salt
Parsley

While the rice cooks, heat the Louisiana Red Sauce. Just before serving, add the scallops to the sauce and simmer until tender, about 5 minutes. Do not overcook. Season to taste with hot sauce and salt.

To serve, spoon some rice in the bottom of each individual soup bowl. Ladle the scallops and sauce on top. Garnish with parsley and serve at once.

Yield: 4–6 servings

Stir Fried Vegetables

1 tablespoon sesame oil
¾ cup raw cashews
2 tablespoons sesame oil
1 teaspoon salt
2 garlic cloves, slivered
1 cup diced green peppers
1 cup diagonally sliced carrots
½ cup diagonally sliced celery
3 cups slivered Chinese cabbage
1 cup fresh or frozen shelled peas
   or snow peas
½ cup diagonally sliced scallions
½ cup Hot Sesame Salsa (page 38)

In a wok or large skillet, heat 1 tablespoon sesame oil. Add the cashews and stir fry until the cashews are browned. Remove from the wok and set aside.

Add the remaining 2 tablespoons sesame oil to the wok and heat until it is just about to smoke. Add the salt and garlic. Remove the garlic when it is browned. Then add the peppers, carrots, and celery. Stir fry for 1 minute, until barely tender. Add the cabbage and stir fry to coat the vegetables in the oil. Add the peas, scallions, and salsa and stir fry until hot, but barely tender, about 2 minutes. Do not overcook. Serve at once with rice.

Yield: 4 servings

Sesame Chicken with Noodles

1 pound boned and
  skinned chicken breasts
1 cup Hot Sesame Salsa (page 38)
1 tablespoon peanut oil
¼ cup sesame seeds
½ pound rice noodles
1 tablespoon peanut oil
1 tablespoon peanut oil
2 cups julienne-sliced green beans
1 cup julienne sliced carrots
½ cup diced hot pepper
2 cups diced sweet green bell pepper
1–2 tablespoons soy sauce or tamari
2 tablespoons chopped scallions

Rice noodles are lighter than wheat noodles and are available at Oriental food stores. If you cannot locate rice noodles, substitute a very thin spaghetti, such as cappellini (angel hair).

Slice the chicken into bite-size pieces. Combine with the salsa. Cover and refrigerate for 2–3 hours to marinate. Stir occasionally.

Heat 1 tablespoon peanut oil in a wok or large skillet. Add the sesame seeds and stir fry until the seeds are golden brown, about 5 minutes. Set aside.

Prepare the rice noodles according to the package directions. Keep warm.

Heat 1 tablespoon oil in the wok and stir fry the chicken with the marinade until the chicken is cooked through, about 5 minutes. Set aside in a warmed bowl and keep warm.

Heat the remaining 1 tablespoon oil. Add

the beans and carrots and stir fry until just barely coated with oil. Add the hot pepper and sweet pepper. Stir fry until the vegetables are bright in color and still very crunchy, about 1 minute. Add 1 tablespoon soy sauce. Then add the chicken and marinade and sesame seeds. Stir fry until everything is heated through, about 1 minute. Season to taste with more soy sauce, if needed.

Serve on a warmed platter with a bed of rice noodles on the bottom and the chicken and vegetables on top. Sprinkle the scallions on top to garnish and serve immediately.

Yield: 4 servings

Couscous Stuffed Eggplant

1½ **pounds eggplant**
Oil
1 cup couscous
2 cups boiling water
½ **pound sausage meat**
   or ¼ **cup olive oil**
1 onion, diced
1 celery rib, diced
6 ounces feta cheese, crumbled
   (about 1½ **cups)**
1½ **cups Harissa Sauce (page 34)**
Salt

The ingredients in this recipe are mostly North African, inspired by the Moroccan Harissa Sauce, which flavors the eggplant filling. The half-pound of sausage adds flavor, but it isn't really necessary.

I buy couscous at my local natural foods coop. It can be found in specialty food stores as well.

Preheat the oven to 425° F.

Slice the eggplant in half. Run a knife along the sides of the eggplant, about ½ inch from the skin. Brush with oil. Set the eggplant, skin side down, in a baking dish. Add about ½ inch of water to the bottom of the dish. Bake for 35–40 minutes, until the eggplant is just tender.

While the eggplant bakes, prepare the couscous by combining the couscous with the boiling water in a bowl. Stir once, cover, and set aside.

When the eggplant is just tender, remove from the oven and reduce the oven temperature to 325° F. Scoop out the flesh, dice, and set aside. Reserve the skins.

In a large skillet, brown the sausage. As the meat browns, break it up with a spoon. Remove the meat to a mixing bowl, and drain off all but ¼ cup fat. Heat the sausage fat, or the olive oil, and sauté the diced eggplant until tender, about 5 minutes. Add the onion and celery and sauté until the onion appears translucent, about 2 more minutes.

Drain off as much fat or oil as possible. Add the vegetables to the sausage meat. Fluff the couscous with a fork and add to the vegetables. Mix in about 1 cup of the cheese, reserving the remainder to sprinkle on top. Mix in the Harissa Sauce. Season to taste with salt.

Stuff the filling into the eggplant skins. Sprinkle the remaining cheese on top. Set the filled eggplant halves in a baking dish. Bake for 20 minutes or until heated through. Serve at once.

Yield: 4 servings

Eggplant Salsa Casserole

2 (1-pound) eggplants
2 cups flour
3 eggs
¾ cup milk
3 cups bread crumbs
1 tablespoon dried oregano
1 teaspoon salt
Oil for frying
2 cups crumbled feta cheese
   (8 ounces)
8 ounces mozzarella, sliced
3 cups Pickled Pepper Salsa
   (page 18) or Jalapeño Salsa
   (page 22)

A flavorful variation on the old favorite: Eggplant Parmesan.

Peel the eggplant and slice about ¼ inch thick. Set out 3 shallow bowls in an assembly line. In the first bowl, place the flour. In the second bowl, beat together the eggs and milk. In the third bowl, combine the bread crumbs, oregano, and salt. At the end of the line, place a few sheets of waxed paper to hold the breaded eggplant.

To bread the eggplant, first dip each slice in the flour, then in the egg mixture, and finally in the bread crumbs.

Preheat about 1 inch of oil in a heavy skillet. Fry each eggplant slice until golden on both sides. Drain well. Add more oil as needed.

Preheat the oven to 375° F.

To assemble the casserole, layer the eggplant, salsa, and cheeses in a 9-inch by 13-

inch baking dish. Continue layering until everything is used. You should end with a cheese layer. Bake for 45 minutes, until the cheese is melted and bubbling and the casserole is hot. Allow the casserole to sit for about 5 minutes before serving.

Yield: 6–8 servings

Cheesy Salsa Pizza

1 tablespoon dry baker's yeast

⅔ cup warm water

¼ teaspoon sugar

1 tablespoon oil

½ teaspoon salt

2 cups sifted all-purpose flour

Cornmeal

2 eggs

2 cups ricotta

1 tablespoon dried oregano

2–3 tomatoes, sliced

½ green pepper, julienne-sliced

½ Spanish onion, thinly sliced

1½ cups Mild Red Chile Chipotle
Salsa (page 24), Pickled Pepper
Salsa (page 18), Jalapeño Salsa
(page 22), or Salsa Marinara (page 87)

½ cup chopped black olives

2 cups crumbled feta cheese
(8 ounces)

2 cups grated mozzarella

This pizza is very rich and filling. A less extravagent variation is offered, too.

First, make the crust. Combine the yeast, warm water, and sugar in a large mixing bowl. Stir to dissolve the yeast, then set aside until the yeast foams, about 5 minutes.

Beat in the oil, salt, and flour. Knead for 10 minutes on a lightly floured surface. Place the dough in a lightly oiled bowl, cover, and let rise for 2 hours.

Preheat the oven to 400° F. Grease a 15-inch cookie sheet or 12-inch pizza pan. Lightly dust with cornmeal. Stretch the dough to fit the pan. Make a rim around the edge of the pan with the dough. Let the dough rest for 10 minutes. Then bake for 10 minutes. (Prebaking prevents the crust from becoming soggy.)

In a mixing bowl, beat the eggs. Add the ricotta and oregano and mix well. Spread evenly over the prebaked crust. Arrange the tomatoes, green peppers, and onion over the ricotta. Spoon the salsa over the vegetables. Sprinkle with the olives, then the feta cheese, then the mozzarella. Bake for 20–25 minutes, until the crust is browned, and the cheese is melted and golden. Allow to stand for 5–10 minutes before slicing.

Yield: 4–5 servings

Variation

Salsa Pizza. Omit the ricotta and eggs. Spoon the salsa over the prebaked crust. Then layer the vegetables, the olives, the feta cheese, and mozzarella on top. Bake as directed above.

Three Cheese Salsa Frittata

¼–½ cup bread crumbs
1 pound cream cheese at room
   temperature
3 eggs
1 cup grated Swiss or Gruyère cheese
1 cup grated cheddar cheese
2 tablespoons flour
2 cups diced sweet red and green
   bell peppers
1 cup Mild Red Chile Chipotle
   (page 24), Hot Red Chile Chipotle
   (page 25), or Vegetable Salsa
   (page 40)

Preheat the oven to 350° F. Butter a 9-inch springform pan and sprinkle with the bread crumbs. Shake the pan to evenly coat with the bread crumbs.

In the mixing bowl of a food processor, or in a regular mixing bowl, beat together the cream cheese and eggs until the mixture is smooth.

In a large mixing bowl, toss the grated cheeses with the flour. Add the cream cheese mixture, peppers, and salsa. Stir until well mixed. Pour into the prepared springform pan. Smooth the top with a knife or spatula.

Bake for 40 minutes, or until the frittata is set. Turn off the oven and allow the frittata to sit in the oven for 10–15 minutes. This can help prevent the top from cracking.

Before serving, run a knife along the inside edge of the pan, then release the sides of the pan. Cut into wedges and serve warm.

Yield: 6–8 servings

Potato Spinach Soufflé

3 cups cubed raw potatoes
3 tablespoons butter
¼ cup milk
1 tablespoon butter
2 garlic cloves, minced
6 cups trimmed raw spinach
3 egg yolks
1 cup cottage cheese
½ cup Vegetable Salsa (page 40)
  or ¾ cup Mild Red Chile Chipotle
  Salsa (page 24)
1 tablespoon Really Hot Pepper
  Sauce (page 30) or Tabasco sauce
3 egg whites

Preheat the oven to 350° F.

Boil the potatoes in water to cover until very tender, 10–12 minutes. Drain. Mash well with a fork. Beat in the 3 tablespoons butter and the milk. Set aside.

Melt 1 tablespoon butter in a large pot. Add the garlic and spinach. Stir until the spinach is well coated with the butter. Then cover and steam until the spinach is wilted, 3–4 minutes. Drain. Squeeze out an excess water. Add to the potatoes. Beat together the egg yolks, cottage cheese, salsa, and hot sauce. Mix into the potatoes.

In another bowl, beat the egg whites until stiff. Fold about one-third of the whites into the potatoes. Then carefully fold the remaining whites into the potatoes. Pour into a greased 2-quart soufflé or baking dish. Bake for 45–50 minutes, until the soufflé is puffed and golden brown. Serve at once.

Yield: 4–6 servings

Zucchini Fritters

4 cups grated zucchini
1 teaspoon salt
1 cup all-purpose unbleached flour
1 teaspoon baking powder
1 teaspoon salt
½ teaspoon dried oregano
½ cup grated cheese
  (cheddar is recommended)
3 eggs
½ cup Little Chicago Salsa (page 28)
½ cup chopped scallion
¼ cup chopped fresh hot pepper
  (optional)
Oil for frying
Little Chicago Salsa (page 28),
  Salsa Cruda (page 16), Jalapeño
  Salsa (page 22), or Avocado Salsa
  Cruda (page 19)
Sour cream

These fritters are great! Even folks who say they don't like zucchini enjoy them. If you are serving to people who aren't enamored with hot foods, skip the hot peppers. The fritters are flavorful, but not hot, with just the salsa.

Ten fritters serve 3 as a main course, and 4–5 as a side dish.

If you like, substitute cooked spaghetti squash or fresh or frozen corn kernals for the zucchini.

Mix the zucchini and salt in a colander. Weight with a heavy plate and let drain for 30 minutes. Squeeze out any additional moisture with your hands.

In a large bowl, sift together the flour, baking powder, and the remaining 1 teaspoon salt. Mix in the oregano and cheese.

In a second bowl, beat the eggs. Add the zucchini, salsa, scallions, and hot pepper.

Add to the flour mixture. Stir just enough to thoroughly mix.

Heat about 1 inch of oil over medium-high heat in a large frying pan. When the oil is hot, drop the batter into the oil, about ¼ cup at a time. Fry until golden on both sides, about 2–3 minutes per side. Drain on paper towels and serve warm. Serve with additional salsa and sour cream on the side.

Yield: 10 fritters

Zucchini Diablo

2 tablespoons olive or safflower oil
2 garlic cloves, minced
4 cups sliced zucchini
2 cups Jalapeño Salsa (page 22),
    Colombian-style Salsa Fria
    (page 23), or Mild Red Chile
    Chipotle Salsa (page 24)
Salt
Sour cream or yogurt (optional)

Just about any vegetable can be substituted for zucchini in this recipe, including okra, green beans, fresh lima beans, corn, cooked dried beans, or cooked spaghetti squash. In fact, just about any sautéed vegetable and any salsa can be combined to make a tasty dish. This zucchini dish makes a wonderful, if nontraditional, filling for enchiladas.

Heat the oil in a large skillet. Add the garlic and zucchini and sauté until the zucchini is barely tender, about 2 minutes. Add the salsa and cook until just heated through. Do not overcook; the zucchini should still be crunchy. Add salt to taste. Serve at once. Pass a bowl of sour cream or yogurt with the zucchini, if desired.

Yield: 4–6 servings

Eggplant Pitas

3 tablespoons vegetable oil
2 teaspoons ground cumin
3 cups diced eggplant
   (1 small eggplant)
2 garlic cloves, minced
1 onion, diced
1 green pepper, diced
3 tablespoons Little Chicago Salsa
   (page 28) or 2 tablespoons Hot
   Red Chile Chipotle Salsa (page 25)
2 cups peeled chopped tomatoes
Salt
4 pita bread pockets
1–2 cups feta cheese, crumbled
   (4–8 ounces)
Sour cream or yogurt
Chopped lettuce

In a large skillet or heavy-bottomed saucepan, heat the oil. Add the cumin and eggplant and sauté for about 7 minutes, until the eggplant is quite tender. If the eggplant sticks to the bottom of the pan, do not add more oil. Cover the pan and let the eggplant steam for a minute or two. Stir well. When the eggplant is tender, add the garlic, onion, and green pepper. Sauté until the onion is translucent, 2–3 minutes. Add the salsa and tomatoes, and sauté for another minute. Then reduce the heat, cover, and simmer for 15 minutes. The vegetables should be quite tender and the flavors blended.

Serve the eggplant mixture hot or at room temperature. Assemble the pita pockets at the table, passing bowls of the eggplant, the cheese, the sour cream or yogurt, and the lettuce.

Yield: 4 servings

Salsa Bean Pot

2 cups great northern beans
2 quarts water
½ pound salt pork (optional)
½ cup maple syrup
1 cup Mild or Hot Chile Chipotle
  Salsa (pages 24-25) or Little Chicago
  Salsa (page 28)
1½ teaspoons dried mustard

An old Yankee favorite given a new twist—sweet *and* hot.

Rinse the beans. Place the beans in a large pot and cover with the water. Bring to a boil and boil for about 2 minutes. Cover, reduce the heat, and simmer for about 1 hour, until the beans are very tender. Drain, saving the water.

Partially slice through the salt pork every ½ inch or so, leaving the rind intact. Place the salt pork in the bottom of a bean pot. Add the drained beans. Combine the maple syrup, salsa, and mustard with 1 cup of the bean water. Pour over the beans. Add more water to cover the beans, if necessary. Cover the pot and bake for 6–8 hours at 250° F. Check occasionally, and add more water if necessary. This is delicious served with corn bread.

Yield: 4–6 servings

Red Beans and Corn

1½ cups dried pinto beans
Water to cover
1 tablespoon oil
1 onion, diced
1 cup Little Chicago Salsa (page 28)
6 cups water
½ teaspoon salt
2 bay leaves
1 tablespoon Really Hot Pepper
   Sauce (page 30)
2 cups fresh shelled or frozen corn

These beans are good for using as a filling for empanadas (see page 50)

Combine the dried beans with water to cover and soak overnight. Drain.

In a large pot, heat the oil. Sauté the onion until slightly tender, 2–3 minutes. Add the beans and the salsa, 6 cups water, salt, bay leaves, and Hot Pepper Sauce. Bring to a boil, reduce the heat, and simmer, partially covered, for about 3 hours, or until the beans are tender. About 10 minutes before serving, stir in the corn. Serve hot over rice.

Yield: 4 servings

Beans and Winter Squash

1½ cups dried black beans
  or any red beans
Water to cover
1 tablespoon oil
2 jalapeños, finely diced
2 garlic cloves, minced
½ cup Mild Red Chile Chipotle
  Salsa (page 24) and ½ cup Barbecue Sauce (page 34) or 1 cup of
  either sauces
6 cups water
1 teaspoon salt
1½–2 cups diced peeled winter
  squash (butternut is recommended
  because it is easy to peel)

I think the flavor is best when this is made with black beans, but the color is best with red beans. In any case, these beans are delicious on a cold day. Serve with fresh corn bread or rice.

Combine the beans with water to cover and soak overnight. Drain.

In a large pot, heat the oil. Sauté the jalapeños and garlic until the jalapeños are tender, about 2 minutes. Add the beans, salsa, 6 cups water, and salt. Simmer for about 2½ hours, until the beans are tender. Add the winter squash and simmer for 30 minutes more. Taste and adjust seasoning. This dish improves with age.

Yield: 4 servings

Ecuador Black Beans

2 cups black beans (turtle beans)
Water to cover
2 tablespoons olive oil
4 garlic cloves, minced
2 medium-size onions, diced
2 tablespoons ground cumin
½–1 cup Little Chicago Salsa
(page 28)
12 cups water
1 teaspoon salt or more to taste

Soak the beans overnight in plenty of water. If you forget to soak overnight, you can soften the beans using the quick soak method: Combine the beans with plenty of water to cover. Bring to a boil. Boil for 10 minutes. Remove from the heat and let sit for at least 1 hour. Then proceed with the recipe.

Drain the beans, reserving the soaking water if desired.

In a large pot, heat the olive oil. Add the garlic, onions, and cumin, and sauté until the onions are tender, 3–5 minutes. Add the salsa, beans, and 12 cups water (which can include soaking water if desired). Bring to a boil, then simmer for 3–4 hours, partially covered, until the liquid is mostly absorbed and the beans are tender. Add more water if necessary as the beans cook. The final consistency should be of firm beans in a thick gravy. Before serving, add salt to taste.

Yield: 6 servings

Mystery Rice

2 tablespoons oil
1 teaspoon ground cumin
1 teaspoon ground chili powder
1 teaspoon salt
2 cups white rice
1 cup salsa
2¼ cups boiling water
Chopped black olives or scallions
  (optional)

Inevitably, my refrigerator fills up with odds and ends of various salsas. This variation on Spanish rice can be made with whatever leftover salsas you happen to have on hand. It works best with chunky-style salsas.

In a large heavy skillet, heat the oil. Add the spices, salt, and rice. Sauté for about 3 minutes, until the rice is well coated with the spices. Add the salsa and boiling water, stir once, cover, and cook for about 20 minutes. The water should be evaporated and the rice tender. Fluff with a fork and serve. Garnish with chopped black olives or chopped scallions, if desired.

Yield: 4 servings

MEXICAN DELIGHTS

Tacos

As with many foods, tacos vary by region. Most of us think of tacos as filled crispy hard corn tortillas. Soft tacos are also fairly common, though some people call soft tacos enchiladas. Soft tacos are made with a soft corn tortilla, folded around a filling and eaten immediately. Enchiladas are baked.

Tacos are usually assembled right at the table. At the table, provide taco shells, plenty of shredded lettuce, chopped onions, chopped tomatoes, shredded cheese, sour cream, and plenty of salsa. Guacamole (page 45) goes well with tacos, too. Here is a list of some fillings that are delicious in tacos.

Fillings

- Refried Beans (page 119)
- Red Beans and Corn (page 105)
- Ecuador Black Beans (page 107)
- Beans and Winter Squash (page 106)
- Barbecued Skewered Vegetables (page 74)
- Red Chicken (from recipe with Yellow Rice, (page 84)
- Shredded Pork (Empanada filling, page 50)
- Shredded Beef (Chimichangas filling, page 120)

Tacos

- Cooked shredded chicken or turkey, heated in a salsa, such as Red Chile Chipotle Salsa (page 24)
- Guacamole (page 45), chopped tomatoes, shredded cheese

Recommended Salsas

- Salsa Cruda (page 16)
- Pickled Pepper Salsa (page 18)
- Tomatillo Salsa (page 20)
- Jack Frost Salsa (page 21)
- Jalapeño Salsa (page 22)
- Colombian-style Salsa Fria (page 23)
- Red Chile Chipotle Salsa (page 24)
- Tomatillo and Chile Chipotle Salsa (page 27)
- Little Chicago Salsa (page 28)
- Mild Hot Pepper Sauce (page 32)
- Harissa Sauce (page 36)
- Vegetable Salsa (page 40)

Burritos

Burritos are large flour tortillas, rolled around a hot filling and served at once or grilled to heat through. They are closely related to chimichangas, which are burritos that are rolled, sealed, and deep-fried (see page 120).

Flour tortillas are found in most supermarkets. Look for them in the dairy case, in the freezer case, or at the meat counter. Where you have a choice, buy the large size tortillas (12–18 inches). These will let you roll to completely encase the filling. The smaller tortillas are rolled with the ends left open—which means you are bound to lose some of the filling out of the open end.

The tortillas should be soft and warm before they are rolled to prevent cracking. If the tortillas feel dry to the touch, sprinkle a few drops of water on each side. Then heat them. Traditionally, tortillas are heated on a comal, or griddle, turned frequently, for about 1 minute. If you don't have a griddle, wrap the tortillas in a tea towel and steam over simmering water for about 5 minutes. Or steam over boiling water for 1 minute. Don't let the tortillas touch the water directly. Or, wrap the tortillas in foil, place the foil pack on a baking sheet or baking dish, and heat in a 350° F. oven for about 15 minutes.

The burritos can be filled with hot meats, beans, or eggs. These hot fillings can be mixed with salsas, chopped onions, chopped tomatoes, shredded cheese, and sour cream. Burritos should be served with plenty of salsa on the side. Garnish with shredded lettuce, chopped onions, and sour cream.

Burritos

Fillings

- Refried Beans (page 119), chopped onions, and grated cheese or sour cream
- Red Beans and Corn (page 105) and grated cheese or sour cream
- Black Beans and Winter Squash (page 106) and grated cheese or sour cream
- Ecuador Black Beans (page 107), chopped onions, and grated cheese or sour cream
- Shredded Pork (Empanada filling, page 50), chopped tomatoes, chopped onions, and sour cream
- Shredded Beef (Chimichanga filling, page 120), chopped tomatoes, chopped onions, and sour cream
- Scrambled eggs, fried potatoes, chopped fresh chiles, and salsa
- Scrambled eggs, Zucchini Diablo (page 102), and sour cream

Recommended Salsas

- See list on page 110. There is one other appropriate salsa, Mild or Hot Chile Chipotle Salsa, pages 24 and 25.

Enchiladas

Enchiladas are filled corn tortillas that are smothered in a sauce and baked to heat through and melt the cheese that is usually a part of the filling.

The corn tortillas should be softened before they are rolled. Heat a little oil in a large skillet. Holding the tortilla with a pair of tongs, dip the tortillas in the hot oil for a few seconds on each side. Drain on paper towels. Spoon a few tablespoons of filling on the center of the tortilla and tightly roll the tortilla, leaving the ends open. Place seam side down in a baking dish or individual serving plates. (Since the enchiladas do not always hold their shape well when lifted from the baking dish, I prefer to heat enchiladas on earthenware dinner plates.) Pour the sauce on top, top with grated cheese, if desired, and bake for about 15 minutes, until the cheese is melted, and the enchiladas are heated through. Garnish the individual serving plates with chopped lettuce, chopped tomatoes, guacamole or avocado slices, orange slices, heated refried beans, and warm rice.

Fillings

- Shredded cheese (cheddar, Swiss, jack, or a combination), chopped onions, sour cream
- Shredded pork (Empanada filling, page 50) and grated cheese or sour cream
- Shredded beef (Chimichanga filling, page 120) and grated cheese or sour cream

Enchiladas

- Shredded cooked turkey or chicken simmered in salsa, chopped green peppers, chopped onions, and sour cream
- Cooked baby shrimp simmered in salsa, chopped green peppers, chopped fresh chiles, and sour cream
- Zucchini Diablo (page 102), chopped onions, and grated cheese or sour cream
- Refried beans (page 119), chopped onions, and grated cheese or sour cream
- Red Beans and Corn (page 105) and grated cheese or sour cream
- Ecuador Black Beans (page 107), chopped onions, and sour cream

Recommended Salsas

- Busy Person's Salsa (page 17)
- Pickled Pepper Salsa (page 18)
- Jalapeño Salsa (page 22)
- Enchilada Salsa Borracha (page 26)
- Mild or Hot Red Chile Chipotle Salsa (pages 24-25)
- Harissa Sauce (page 36)

Quesadillas

There's plenty of regional differences to consider when describing what goes into a making a quesadilla. It can be made with a flour or corn tortilla. They can be served open-faced or rolled. They may be grilled or baked or fried. I prefer to make quesadillas with flour tortillas rolled around a filling, then grilled or baked. There is a recipe for Cheese Quesadillas on page 122. Any filling that you might use for a burrito will be delicious in a quesadilla.

Eggs

Eggs without salsa seems incomplete to me. I rarely even serve eggs without passing salsa on the side. A teaspoon or so of salsa usually goes into the scrambled eggs. I make deviled eggs with mayonnaise and salsa.

Here's a few recipe ideas for egg and salsa combinations.

Richard Ruane's Mexican Omelet. Beat 2–3 eggs well. Add 2 tablespoons salsa and beat well. Melt 2 teaspoons butter in a well-seasoned omelet pan over medium high heat. Pour the eggs into the butter when it foams. Sprinkle ¼–½ cup grated Swiss, Gruyère, or cheddar cheese on the eggs. When the eggs have set, fold the omelet in half, continue cooking for about 1 minute. Serve at once, preferably with fried potatoes, and pass plenty of salsa on the side.

Huevos Rancheros. There's plenty of variations for making this dish. Here's my method.

Begin by preheating the oven to 300° F. Heat refried beans and salsa. For each serving, soften 1 corn tortilla by dipping it in hot oil in a skillet and cooking just long enough to soften. Drain on paper towels. On each individual serving plate, place a corn tortilla. Top with refried beans and salsa. Keep the plates warm in the oven while you prepare the eggs. The eggs can be scrambled, poached in water or salsa, or fried. Place the eggs on top of the assembled corn tortillas and serve at once. Pass additional salsa and sour cream. Fried potatoes go well with huevos rancheros.

Mexican Frittata. A combination of ideas . . .

Melt 2 tablespoons of butter in a medium-size frying pan. Add about 1 cup of chopped vegetables — onions, green peppers, zucchini or summer squash, green beans, for example — and sauté for a minute or 2. Add about ¼ cup of salsa and continue to sauté until the vegetables are barely tender, another minute or two. Sprinkle about ½ cup of grated cheddar, Gruyère, or Swiss cheese on top of the vegetables. Beat together 2 eggs and hot sauce to taste. Pour the eggs over the vegetables and cheese. Cover. Bake in a preheated 350° F. oven for about 2 minutes, until the eggs are set. Serve at once.

Chilaquiles

I've eaten chilaquiles that were called Mexican tortes. Whatever the name, they are easy to prepare and delicious. Basically a chilaquiles is a layered casserole, made up of tortilla strips, salsa, cheese, and, sometimes, meat or beans.

To make a chilaquiles, first preheat the oven to 350° F. Then soften about 6 tortillas by dipping them in hot oil for 1 minute on the first side, and 30 seconds on the second side. Cut the tortillas into strips with a pair of kitchen scissors or a sharp knife.

Assemble your ingredients: plenty of grated cheese, some salsa or sautéed tomatoes and chiles, tortilla strips, and whatever else suits your fancy. Spoon a little salsa onto the bottom of a 2-quart baking dish. Place a layer of tortilla strips, then a layer of meat or beans or vegetables, then salsa, then cheese. Keep repeating the layers until all is used, ending with a layer of cheese. Bake for about 30 minutes, until the cheese is melted and golden. Allow the casserole to sit for about 5 minutes before serving.

Recommended Combinations

- Grated cheddar cheese, Salsa Cruda (page 16) or Jalapeño Salsa (page 22) or Pickled Pepper Salsa (page 18), and sautéed sweet bell pepper strips and hot pepper strips
- Grated cheese, feta cheese, and salsa
- Browned beef or sausage, Red Chile Chipotle Salsa (page 24), and grated cheese
- Refried beans, salsa, and cheese
- For a recipe for Sausage Chilaquiles, see page 124

Refried Beans

1½ cups pinto beans
Water to cover
5 cups water
¼ cup **Little Chicago Salsa** (page 28)
4 bay leaves
1 teaspoon salt
2 tablespoons oil
2 garlic clove, minced
1 teaspoon chile powder
1 teaspoon ground cumin

Combine the beans and water to cover. Let soak overnight. Or, combine the beans and water in a large saucepan. Bring to a boil and boil for 10 minutes. Set aside to soak for 1 hour.

Drain the beans and reserve the soaking water if desired. In a large saucepan, combine the beans with 5 cups of water (which can include the soaking water). Bring to a boil, then simmer, partially covered for 2–2½ hours, until the beans are very tender.

Heat the oil in a large skillet. Add the garlic, chile powder, and cumin and sauté until the spices foam, about 2 minutes. Add the beans and break the beans up with a spoon or mash with a potato masher. The mixture should be fairly chunky. Simmer for about ½ hour, until the liquid has mostly evaporated and the beans have a smooth consistency. Serve hot.

Yield: 4 servings

Chimichangas

2 tablespoons oil
4 tablespoons chili powder
2 garlic cloves
1-pound chuck stew meat
Water to cover
½ cinnamon stick
1 teaspoon dried oregano
1 teaspoon whole allspice
1 teaspoon salt
½ teaspoon black pepper
Oil for deep frying
8 large flour tortillas
About 3 tablespoons Little Chicago
    Salsa (page 28)
1 cup sour cream

Chimichangas are deep-fried burritos. The beef filling here can be used in regular burritos, empanadas, or tacos.

In a heavy saucepan, heat the oil. Add the chili powder and garlic and cook until the chili powder foams, about 2 minutes. Add the stew meat and brown the meat, stirring frequently, for about 10 minutes. Add water to cover, the cinnamon stick, oregano, allspice, salt, and pepper. Simmer until the meat is very tender, about 2 hours. Cover the pot for the first hour of cooking, then remove the cover and let the cooking liquid reduce. The meat should be tender enough so that you can easily shred it with a fork.

Heat the oil in a deep pot to 350° F. While the oil heats, roll the chimichangas. First steam the tortillas over boiling water for about 1 minute each. This softens the tortillas and makes them easy to handle. Fill each tortilla with about 3 tablespoons of shredded meat. Spoon about 1 teaspoon of the salsa on the meat, and top with about 1 tablespoon of sour cream. Roll the tortilla as you would an eggroll (see page 46) and secure with 2 toothpicks.

When the oil is hot, fry the rolled tortillas, 1 at a time, for about 2 minutes each. Drain and serve at once. Pass extra salsa and sour cream.

Yield: 4 servings

Variations

Pork Chimichangas. Substitute pork for the beef and proceed with the recipe above.

Bean Chimichangas. Substitute Ecuador Black Beans (page 107) or Refried Beans (page 119) for the beef.

Quesadillas

1 cup Tomatillo and Chile Chipotle
  Salsa (page 27)
¼ cup sour cream
6–8 flour tortillas
4 cups grated cheddar, Gruyère,
  or Monterey jack cheese
1 sweet green or red bell pepper,
  diced
1 onion, diced
1 fresh hot pepper, diced
1 avocado, diced

The flour tortillas you use in this recipe come in different sizes depending on what brand you buy. So figure that the ingredient measures are approximate and fill the tortillas with a "reasonable" amount of filling.

Combine the salsa and sour cream and set aside.

Lightly grease a large, heavy skillet and heat over medium-high heat. Lay 1 tortilla down in the center of the skillet. Sprinkle about ½ cup of cheese onto the tortilla to completely cover the surface. Over the cheese, sprinkle some of the sweet pepper, onion, hot pepper, and avocado. Fold the tortilla into thirds, folding the 2 sides of the tortilla over the middle, as you might fold a crêpe. Carefully flip the tortilla over, and cook until the cheese is melted, about 1 minute. Remove the tortilla from the heat and keep warm while you make the remaining quesadillas. I like to set the quesadillas on earthernware dinner plates and set the plates in a warm (250° F.) oven until I am ready to serve. Serve the quesadillas smothered in the tomatillo and sour cream sauce. Fill the plates with garnishes of chopped lettuce and tomatoes, olives, sliced avocados, etc.

Yield: 3-4 servings

Sausage Chilaquiles

1 pound hot Italian sausage
1 tablespoon oil
6 corn tortillas
2½–3 cups Harissa Sauce (page 36)
3–4 cups grated sharp cheddar
   cheese

The combination of flavors in this dish—inspired by leftovers in the refrigerator—works so well I had to include the recipe. Find more ideas for chilaquiles, including a vegetarian version on page 118.

Preheat the oven to 350° F.

Slice open the sausage casings and remove the sausage meat. In a large skillet, brown the sausage, breaking it up with a spoon as it cooks. Drain and set aside.

Heat 1 tablespoon oil in a skillet, briefly fry the tortillas in the oil until softened, about 1 minute on the first side and 30 seconds on the second side. Cut the tortillas into strips. A kitchen scissors does this job well.

Spoon a little sauce into the bottom of a 2-quart baking dish. Arrange a layer of tortilla strips on top. Then layer on some sausage, then a generous coating of cheese. Repeat the layers until all the ingredients are used, ending with a layer of cheese. Bake for 30 minutes until the cheese is melted and golden. Allow the casserole to sit for about 5 minutes before serving. Pass extra salsa and sour cream at the table.

GLOSSARY OF
SELECTED INGREDIENTS

There are no unusual ingredients in this cookbook—if you are familiar with Mexican foods. If not, this glossary is for you.

Achiote (a-chee-o-tay). These are the seeds of the annatto tree (*Bixa Orellana*). Used in flavoring both Mexican and Caribbean foods, these small brick-red seeds give a saffron yellow color and a very fragrant, rich flavor to foods, especially rice. You can buy the seeds dried (look for either annatto or achiote seeds) or crushed. The flavoring also is available as a commercially packaged paste, made with achiote seeds, peppercorns, vinegar, salt, and garlic. I find the paste more convenient to use than the seeds.

Beans. All of the beans used in this cookbook are dried. They are readily found in most supermarkets and natural foods stores. Black beans are also know as turtle beans. A variety of beans can be used in dishes calling for red beans including, red kidney beans, pinto beans, cranberry beans, pink beans.

Chiles. See pages 2-10.

Cilantro (see-lan-tro). Also called fresh coriander or Chinese parsley, this herb is used frequently in salsas. You use the leaves of the plant, and these resemble Italian parsley—in appearance, not in flavor. The flavor is very pungent, almost perfume-like. Not everyone likes the flavor of cilantro, so use it sparingly (I often omit it). It tastes like it smells, so if you like the smell, you'll like the flavor.

Cilantro grows very easily from seed. Care for it as you would parsley. Unfortunately, dried cilantro cannot be substituted for the fresh as it loses too much flavor. Cilantro is often available fresh wherever Mexican, Carribean, Indian, or Chinese foods are sold. If possible, buy the fresh herb with the roots intact. Remove any wilted or yellowed leaves. Set the bunch in a tall glass partially filled with water to keep the roots moist. Cover the leaves with a plastic bag and store in the refrigerator. The herb should remain fresh for about 1 week.

Masa Harina. A commercially prepared dehydrated corn flour, Masa Harina is usually used to make tortillas and tamales.

Tomatillo (to-ma-tee-yo). Also called tomates verdes, tomatillos are small tart husk tomatoes. Although they are from the same family as cape gooseberries and ground cherries, tomatillos are tarter, with a lemony flavor. Canned tomatillos are available where Mexican foods are sold, and can be ordered through the mail from many of the suppliers listed on pages 128-130.

MAIL ORDER
SOURCES OF INGREDIENTS

If you don't happen to live near a large city, or in an area where there is a large Hispanic population, you may have trouble finding ingredients required for some of the recipes. Fortunately there are many companies that sell these foods by mail.

Listed here are suppliers with whom I have dealt. There are probably many other suppliers. Shop around. The prices vary widely.

Dried Chiles, Canned Chiles, and Seasonings

Albuquerque Traders
PO Box 10171
Albuquerque, NM 87114

Ashley's Inc.
6590 Montana Ave.
El Paso, TX 79925

Casa Moneo
210 W. 14th St.
New York, NY 10011
Catalog: $2.00
Minimum order: $25.00

Casados Farms
PO Box 1269
San Juan Pueblo, NM 87566
Price list: $1.00

El Molina
117 S. 22nd St.
Phoenix, AZ 85034

Herman Valdez Fruit Stand
PO Box 218
Velarde, NM 87582

Los Chileros Inc.
1365-F Rufina Circle
Sante Fe, NM 87501

Mexican Chile Supply
304 E. Belknap St.
Fort Worth, TX 76102

Mexican Kitchen
Box 213
Brownsville, TX 78520

Pecos Valley Spice Company
186 Fifth Avenue
New York, NY 10010

H. Roth & Sons
1577 First Ave.
New York, NY 10021

Sasabe Store
PO Box 7
Sasabe, AZ 85633
Catalog: $1.00. Refundable
with first purchase

Tia Mia
720 N. Walnut
El Paso, TX 79903

Chile Seeds

(For growing chiles in your garden)

Guerney's Seed and Nursery Company
Yankton, SD 57079

Horticultural Enterprises
PO Box 810082
Dallas, TX 75381

Johnny's Selected Seeds
Albion, ME 04910

Nichol's Garden Nursery
1190 North Pacific Highway
Albany, OR 97321

About the Author

Andrea Chesman is the author of *Pickles and Relishes: 150 Recipes from Apples to Zucchini* (Garden Way Publishing) and *Summer in a Jar: Making Pickles, Jams and More* (Williamson Publishing). She is an editor and a frequent contributor of food articles to a variety of magazines and newspapers. She lives in northern Vermont where the summers are too short to grow a decent crop of hot peppers.

INDEX

NOTES

NOTES

NOTES

NOTES

NOTES